EVERYMAN

J. M. Dent · London

This edition first published by Everyman Paperbacks in 1997

Selection, introduction and other critical apparatus © J. M. Dent 1997

The editor and publishers wish to thank Mrs Myfanwy Thomas for permission to
reprint text from Edward Thomas's *Collected Poems*.

J. M. Dent
Orion Publishing Group
Orion House
5 Upper St Martin's Lane,
London WC2H 9EA

Typeset by Deltatype Ltd, Birkenhead, Merseyside
Printed in Great Britain by
The Guernsey Press Co. Ltd, Guernsey, C.I.

British Library Cataloguing-in-Publication Data
is available upon request.

ISBN 0 460 87877 8

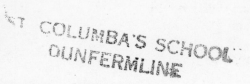

Contents

1917

Note on the Author and Editor

PHILIP EDWARD THOMAS was born in London on 3 March 1878 of Welsh parents. His father, a staff clerk at the Board of Trade, hoped that his son would enter the Civil Service, but Thomas showed early promise as a writer, publishing essays when he was seventeen and his first book before he went up to Oxford. While an undergraduate, he secretly married Helen Noble, and his son was born before he took his degree. Thereafter he determined to live by his pen. In fifteen years he produced more than thirty prose books, sixteen editions or anthologies and over a million words in reviews to support his family, which now included two daughters. Incessant overwork led to severe depression, thoughts of suicide, and in 1911 to a serious breakdown. He described himself as a 'hurried & harried prose man', but in October 1913 he became close friends with the American poet Robert Frost, who recognised and encouraged the poet in Thomas. In December 1914, when he was 'thirty-six in the shade', Thomas suddenly began to write poetry and produced the one hundred and forty-two poems of his *Collected Poems* in two years. During that time he also enlisted and trained as an artillery officer. In January 1917 he embarked for France, where he took up duties in forward observation posts. On 9 April 1917 – Easter Monday – he was killed by the blast of a shell at the beginning of the Battle of Arras.

WILLIAM COOKE lectured for many years before becoming a full-time writer. A biographer, critic, poet and short-story writer, his publications include *Edward Thomas: A Critical Biography* (Faber, 1970). Currently he is working on a new collection of his own poetry.

Chronology of Edward Thomas's Life

Year	Age	Life
1878		3 March: Born at Lambeth, London, to Philip Henry and Mary Elizabeth Thomas. Eldest of six sons (Ernest, Theodore, Reginald, Oscar and Julian)
1883–93	5–15	Attends various schools in London including Battersea Grammar School; holidays spent in Wiltshire and Wales
1894	16	Attends St Paul's School, Hammersmith. Visits the writer and critic James Ashcroft Noble who encourages his literary aspirations
1895	17	Leaves St Paul's. Publishes essays in various periodicals. Friendship with Helen Noble

Chronology of his Times

Year	Literary Context	Historical Events
1878	Hardy, *The Return of the Native*	
1879	Meredith, *The Egoist*	Births of Joseph Stalin and Albert Einstein
1880	Death of George Eliot	First Boer War
1885	Rider Haggard, *King Solomon's Mines*	Death of General Gordon at Khartoum
1886	Birth of Siegfried Sassoon	Gladstone's third Liberal Government introduces Home Rule Bill for Ireland
1887	Death of Richard Jefferies / Birth of Rupert Brooke	Queen Victoria's Golden Jubilee
1889	Conan Doyle, *The Sign of Four*	Birth of Adolf Hitler
1890	Births of Ivor Gurney and Isaac Rosenberg	Parnell resigns from Parliament
1892	Death of Tennyson	Gladstone's fourth ministry
1893	Birth of Wilfred Owen	Independent Labour Party formed
1894	Kipling, *The Jungle Book* / Death of Walter Pater	
1895	Births of Robert Graves and Charles Sorley / Wilde, *The Importance of Being Earnest* (performed)	Salisbury's third ministry; X-rays discovered

Year	Age	Life
1896	18	Death of J. A. Noble. Works initially for Civil Service examination, then for entry to Oxford University
1897	19	Publishes first book, *The Woodland Life*. Oct: Goes up to Oxford where he wins a History scholarship to Lincoln College (1898)
1899	21	June: Marries Helen Noble at Fulham Registry Office
1900	21	Jan: Birth of son, Merfyn
	22	Summer: Gains second-class History degree; starts a precarious and lifelong career as a writer
1901	23	Moves from Balham, London, to Rose Acre Cottage near Bearsted in Kent
1902	24	Publishes *Horae Solitariae*; begins friendship with Gordon Bottomley. Oct: Birth of elder daughter, Bronwen
1903	25	First commissioned book, *Oxford*. The Thomases move to a cottage on Bearsted Green
1904	26	Publishes *Rose Acre Papers*. Moves to Elses Farm in the Weald, near Sevenoaks
1905	27	Publishes *Beautiful Wales*; continues reviewing and writing commissioned books; suffers physical and mental exhaustion. Befriends W.H. Davies
1906	28	Meets W. H. Hudson and Walter de la Mare. Publishes *The Heart of England*. Moves to Berryfield Cottage, Petersfield, Hampshire, close to Bedales School which his children later attend
1907	29	Consults specialist about his 'melancholia'

Year	Literary Context	Historical Events
1896	Birth of Edmund Blunden A. E. Housman, *A Shropshire Lad*	First modern Olympic Games (Athens)
1897	H. G. Wells, *The Invisible Man*	Queen Victoria's Diamond Jubilee
1899	Freud, *The Interpretation of Dreams*	Second Boer War; siege of Mafeking
1900	Conrad, *Lord Jim*	Mafeking relieved
1901		Death of Victoria; accession of Edward VII
1902	De la Mare, *Songs of Childhood* Bennett, *Anna of the Five Towns*	Boer War ends
1903	Butler, *The Way of All Flesh*	Suffragette movement in UK; Wright brothers make first powered flight
1904	J. M. Barrie, *Peter Pan* (performed) Chekhov, *The Cherry Orchard*	
1905	E. M. Forster, *Where Angels Fear to Tread*	
1906	Galsworthy, *The Man of Property*	James Keir Hardie co-founder and first leader of the Labour Party
1907	Synge, *The Playboy of the Western World* Shaw, *Major Barbara*	

Year	Age	Life
1908	30	Aug: Assistant Secretary to a Royal Commission on Welsh Monuments; Dec: resigns, depressed and in ill-health
1909	31	Publishes *Richard Jefferies* and *The South Country*. Moves into 'the new house' at Wick Green, Petersfield
1910	32	Publishes *Windsor Castle, Rest and Unrest, Feminine Influence on the Poets*. Aug: Birth of Myfanwy, his second daughter. Visits Joseph Conrad, Hilaire Belloc and Rupert Brooke
1911	33	Works on six books; publishes *Maurice Maeterlinck*; severe nervous breakdown caused by overwork and financial anxiety; recuperates in Wales
1912	34	Publishes *Lafcadio Hearn, Norse Tales, Algernon Charles Swinburne* and *George Borrow*. Meets Eleanor Farjeon
1913	35	His health deteriorates. Publishes *The Country, The Icknield Way, The Happy-Go-Lucky Morgans* and *Walter Pater*. Moves to Yew Tree Cottage in the village of Steep. Oct: Meets Robert Frost
1914	36	Publishes *In Pursuit of Spring*; reviews Frost's *North of Boston*. Aug: The Thomases and Frosts holiday at Ledington, near Ledbury. Considers leaving with Frost for USA. Dec: Starts to write poetry
1915	36	Feb: Merfyn sails with Frosts for USA visit
	37	July: Enlists in Artists' Rifles. Nov: Map-reading instructor at Hare Hall Camp, Gidea Park, Essex. Publishes *This England*
1916	38	Publishes *Keats*. Sept: Officer cadet at Royal Artillery School, Handel Street, London; moves family to High Beech, Essex. Nov: Commissioned second lieutenant; posted to 244 Siege Battery, Lydd, Kent. Dec: Volunteers for service overseas

Year	Literary Context	Historical Events
1908	W. H. Davies, *The Autobiography of a Supertramp*	Asquith's Liberal Government
1909	Pound, *Personae* Death of Swinburne	Ford's Model T car; old-age pensions first paid
1910	Deaths of Mark Twain and Tolstoy	Death of Edward VII; accession of George V
1911	Rupert Brooke, *Poems 1911* Beerbohm, *Zuleika Dobson*	Amundsen reaches South Pole
1912	*Georgian Poetry 1911–12* Jung, *The Psychology of the Unconscious*	Balkan Wars; loss of *Titanic*; Anglo-German naval talks fail
1913	D. H. Lawrence, *Sons and Lovers* Robert Bridges made Poet Laureate	Woodrow Wilson US President
1914	Joyce, *Dubliners* Yeats, *Responsibilities* Frost, *North of Boston*	28 June: Archduke Franz Ferdinand assassinated; 4 Aug: Britain declares war on Germany
1915	Deaths of Rupert Brooke and Charles Sorley	*Lusitania* sunk by German submarine; Dardanelles expedition; Zeppelin raids
1916	Graves, *Over the Brazier* Joyce, *A Portrait of the Artist as a Young Man*	Battles of Verdun, the Somme, Jutland; Easter Rising, Dublin; Lloyd George Prime Minister

Year	Age	Life
1917	38	Jan: 'Last Poem' written in his diary; embarks from Southampton
	39	March: Publication of *An Annual of New Poetry* containing eighteen of his poems under the pseudonym of Edward Eastaway. Takes up duties at observation post, Beaurains. 4 April: Sees *TLS* review of his poems in *An Annual*. 9 April: Killed by the blast of a shell at the start of the Battle of Arras. 10 April: Buried in the military cemetery at Agny. Oct: *Poems*
1918		*Last Poems* published
1920		*Collected Poems* published

Year	Literary Context	Historical Events
1917	T. S. Eliot, *Prufrock and Other Observations* Kafka, *Metamorphosis*	Russian Revolution; Battles of Arras and Passchendaele; US enters First World War
1918	Deaths of Isaac Rosenberg and Wilfred Owen Rupert Brooke, *Collected Poems* Sassoon, *Counter Attack*	11 Nov: First World War ends
1919	Sassoon, *War Poems*	Treaty of Versailles

Introduction

Edward Thomas's reputation rests on his *Collected Poems*.[1] That we have this volume at all is little short of a miracle, for, apart from suppressed juvenilia, he wrote no poetry until he was nearly thirty-seven. Two years later he was killed in action.

Gordon Bottomley described Thomas's life up to his thirty-sixth year as 'little more than the agony of a swimmer upstream, and in a strong current against which he could scarcely keep his head cleared'.[2] For fifteen years Thomas earned a precarious living by his pen, producing more than thirty books of topography, literary criticism, biography, fiction and sketches, compiling or introducing sixteen editions and anthologies, and writing well over a million words in reviews. Most of this work was commissioned and produced against deadlines. 'I have three books in hand to be done before the year's end,' he wrote to Harold Monro in 1911, 'have written 2 short ones already this year, & have just published one & am about to correct the proofs of another.' Small wonder that in the same year he suffered a severe breakdown or that in 1913 he caricatured himself as a 'doomed hack'. His literary career turned out to be a treadmill that was almost lifelong.

Incessant overwork also created domestic tension, and there were periods of estrangement when he lived apart from his wife and family. Moreover, it intensified his bouts of depression and self-doubt, one consequence of which was contempt for his own work. Of *Oxford* (1903) he wrote: 'Most of it is either dull or drivelling';[3] *Beautiful Wales* (1905) he described as 'sometimes dull, & often unintelligible';[4] *The Heart of England* (1906) was 'Borrow & Jefferies sans testicles & guts'.[5]

Such comments are not the whole truth. While some of his prose is tedious and overwritten, there are fine sections in most of his books, and indeed Thomas spent time and energy including in them prose poems or 'spurred lyrics' that are sometimes the prototypes of later poems. A number of these books were reissued between 1978 and 1984. They included *The South Country* (1909), *The Icknield Way* (1913) and *In Pursuit of Spring* (1914), which are accounts of Thomas's journeys, real and to some extent symbolic passages in his spiritual autobiography foreshadowing major poems that are themselves journeys, pursuits, quests ('The Sign-Post', 'The Other', 'Lob').

However, it was in his criticism that he began to find the right road, the right form. Here is a different Thomas, acute, witty, assured, eminently readable, eminently quotable, whether he is reviewing Lloyd Mifflin ('many of his sonnets are so long that we can scarce believe our eyes which see only 14 lines')[6] or W. B. Yeats ('In reading [*The King's Threshold*], I seem to find, with astonishment, that verse is the natural speech of men, as singing is of birds').[7] His critical works, especially *Maurice Maeterlinck* (1911), *Algernon Charles Swinburne* (1912) and *Walter Pater* (1913), helped exorcise pernicious influences on his own style and acted as the midwife to the poetry. From 1901 onwards, in review after review, critical study after critical study, we hear Thomas eloquently beginning to find his own voice. By the time Robert Frost's *North of Boston* (1914) appeared, his own ideas on style corresponded with those of the American. Thomas's review of *North of Boston* was, essentially, his own poetic manifesto. It began: 'This is one of the most revolutionary books of modern times, but one of the quietest and least aggressive. It speaks, and it is poetry.'[8] As one of the foremost reviewers of his time, Thomas gave Frost standing as a poet; Frost, in turn, recognised and admired the poet in Thomas before he had written a line of poetry, and by his confident example and encouragement helped him fly the 'old nest of prose'.[9] Their brotherhood and the quiet revolution it introduced paralleled that of Wordsworth and Coleridge a century earlier.

In December 1914 Thomas's poetry came in a rush – as if to meet another deadline – and in just over two years he wrote a lifetime's poems. Frost was already urging him to begin afresh in New Hampshire, but ultimately their roads diverged: Frost returned to America, to popular and critical acclaim; Thomas left for France and almost fifty years of neglect.

'Say his poetry has the quality of bread, or tweed, or a ploughed field; strength, simplicity and a natural delicacy that together can express the most complex and mysterious moods – what he called "melancholy" – and at the same time convey a tremendous reality, both of place and time and mind.'[10] Thus Alun Lewis reviewed Thomas's poetry in 1941.

It is significant that this was written by another poet, for although Thomas's poetry is now highly regarded, it initially suffered the neglect that he himself foresaw in 'Aspens' and 'I Never Saw that Land Before'. This, with the notable exception of F. R. Leavis in *New Bearings in English Poetry* (1932), was a critical neglect, for Thomas's *Collected Poems* has been continuously in print since his death, suggesting generations of ordinary readers who have responded 'when such whispers bid'.

One reason was perhaps the difficulty in categorising Thomas's poetry. He has been variously described as a nature poet, a Georgian, a war poet and a modernist, but no single term seems adequate. Although he wrote of nature, the subject is often his own inner nature. He was rejected by the Georgians, then with the Georgians – although Leavis detected a 'distinctly modern sensibility'.[11] His name appeared on the memorial to the poets of the Great War unveiled in Westminster Abbey in 1985, but in the pioneering studies of the literature of that war he was scarcely mentioned. For Thomas wrote no poetry in France, and his war poems are unlike those of his contemporaries. The significance of this aspect of his verse has only gradually been appreciated – by such critics as Edna Longley in *Poetry in the Wars* (1986):[12] 'His images of personal and social upheaval form a war poetry of the Home Front, complementing that of Wilfred Owen.'

Another reason for critical neglect may have been fascination with the life at the expense of the work, much of which has been virtually inaccessible until recently – even a definitive edition of the *Collected Poems* was not available until 1978. Biographies appeared in 1937, 1939, 1970 and 1978 before Professor R. G. Thomas's authorised biography in 1985. However, the first critical study, written by H. Coombes, appeared only in 1956. A few years later, when Vernon Scannell offered to write a pamphlet for the British Council's *Writers and their Work* series, he was told that Thomas did not merit such recognition, although in 1963 the monograph did go ahead. It was not until 1980 that Andrew Motion published the first full-length study devoted entirely to the poetry. Selections from Thomas's prose were made by Roland Gant in 1948 and 1977, and by David Wright in 1981, while Edna Longley's *A Language not to be Betrayed* (1981)[13] was the first selection to give pride of place to his criticism. Volumes of Thomas's letters have also appeared, the latest being his *Selected Letters* (1995).[14]

With the wealth of material now becoming available, it should be possible to answer the final nagging question: Is Thomas a minor or major figure? During the years of neglect he had always been 'a poet's poet', and the virtues extolled by Alun Lewis, together with his technical virtuosity, have fed into the mainstream of British poetry – 'worn new / again and again' – in the work of the thirties' poets Auden, Day-Lewis and Spender, in the Second War poetry of Alun Lewis himself, and more recently in the work of Philip Larkin, R. S. Thomas and Ted Hughes. In 1991 *Elected Friends* (*Poems for and about Edward Thomas*)[15] was published. It contains the work of more than sixty poets, including Walter de la Mare, W. H. Auden, Robert Frost, Ivor Gurney, Dannie Abse, Derek Walcott, Leslie Norris, P. J. Kavanagh, Peter Porter, Michael Longley, Elizabeth Jennings, Norman Nicholson, Geoffrey Grigson, Gavin Ewart, Alan Brownjohn and Elizabeth Bartlett. It is difficult to think of a similar tribute to any other poet, and it is obvious that Thomas continues to have a major influence on twentieth-century poetry.

The order of the poems in this selection is chronological, from the 115 lines of Thomas's first poem to the final twelve lines recovered from his war diary. The dates of the poems are given in the notes and underline his astonishing fluency and development. It was, as John Lehmann wrote in *The Open Night*, 'as if, in the last years of his life, under the stress of war and the desperate sense of urgency it gives to the creative artist who is threatened with annihilation by it, he had recovered the whole range of his inspiration over twenty years, so that he could resume and concentrate it in the new medium'.[16] It is, perhaps, no coincidence that in his third poem, 'March', Thomas portrayed the urgent singing of the thrushes at the onset of night as they strove 'to pack into that hour / Their unwilling hoard of song'.

Broadly the poems fall into two main groups: the first are his pre-enlistment poems, ending with 'For These', completed on the day he was passed fit for military service; the second group deals with his initial reactions to service life and the gradual crystallisation of his decision to volunteer for service overseas.

The first group contains poems which are subtly patriotic, elegiac for the people and places of England that were already passing before the war began to accelerate the process. Thomas included two of them, 'The Manor Farm' and 'Haymaking', in his *This England* (1915) anthology, placing himself in the tradition of writers who had celebrated England in peace and war. Once the aesthete, he now wanted his 'English words' to be 'as dear / As the earth which you prove / That we love' ('Words'). Thomas needed to prove himself by word and deed. The poems here map the road he was to take.

'Lob' stands at the heart of these poems, a cornucopia of English history, legend, folklore, fairy tale, literature and place names – 'as full of English character and country as an egg is of meat'.[17] It is also inevitably a portrait of the artist himself, and just as inevitably it ends with a series of battlefield allusions, for Lob had to be both warrior and sage to protect what he held in trust.

Thomas's imaginative awareness of the suffering and sacrifice of others ('Man and Dog', 'The Owl', 'In Memoriam (Easter, 1915)') concentrated his own internal debate – whether to enlist or accompany Frost to America. This is reflected in such poems as 'The Sign-Post', 'For These', 'I Built Myself a House of Glass' and 'A Dream'. The 'old friend' in the last poem is Frost, and three days after writing it, Thomas told him of his decision to enlist.

Thomas described that decision as 'not at all a desperate nor yet a purposed resolution but the natural culmination of a long series of moods & thoughts'.[18] The same might be said of his decision to volunteer for service overseas, though these moods and thoughts, expressed in the second group of poems, grow perceptibly bleaker ('Rain', 'February Afternoon', 'Gone, Gone Again'). His determination to prove himself inevitably confronts him with the possibility of his own death, and there is in these poems a sense of leave-taking, of people, places and natural phenomena, his group of 'Household Poems' being a poetic will and testament to his wife and family. The road that once led to self-discovery ('The Other') now leads inexorably to France ('Roads') and 'blurs' in the forest of unconsciousness ('Lights Out'). In his penultimate poem he is 'Out in the Dark', on the brink of extinction.

Thomas was killed at his observation post by a stray shell on 9 April 1917. He had survived on the Western Front for sixty-nine days.

WILLIAM COOKE

References

1. Edward Thomas's *Collected Poems* was first published by Selwyn & Blount Ltd (London, 1920): this volume includes *Poems* (London: Selwyn & Blount, 1917), *Last Poems* (London: Selwyn & Blount, 1918) and the poem 'Up in the Wind'. *Two Poems* ('The Lane' and 'The Watchers') was published by Ingpen & Grant (London, 1927). In 1928 Ingpen & Grant published *Collected Poems*: this volume includes the *Collected Poems* of 1920, *Two Poems* (1927), the poems 'No One So Much As You' and 'The Wind's Song'. This collection was reset and first issued by Faber & Faber Ltd in 1936. The poem 'P.H.T.' was included for the first time in their fifth impression of 1949. The text of this edition is based upon the eleventh impression of 1974.

2. Gordon Bottomley, 'A Note on Edward Thomas' in *The Welsh Review*, vol. IV, no. 3 (September 1945), p. 173.

3. Anthony Berridge (ed.), *The Letters of Edward Thomas to Jesse Berridge* (London: Enitharmon Press, 1983), p. 41.

4. R. G. Thomas (ed.), *Letters from Edward Thomas to Gordon Bottomley* (London: Oxford University Press, 1968), p. 77.

5. ibid, p. 107.

6. Edna Longley (ed.), *A Language not to be Betrayed* (Manchester: Carcanet Press, 1981), p. v.

7. ibid, p. 81.

8. Edward Thomas, 'A New Poet' in *The Daily News and Leader*, 22 July 1914, p. 7.

9. Edward Garnett (ed.), Introduction in *Selected Poems* by Edward Thomas (Montgomeryshire: The Gregynog Press, 1927), p. xiii.

10. Alun Lewis, 'Review of *The Trumpet and Other Poems*' in *Horizon*, vol. III, no. 13 (January 1941), p. 80.

11. F. R. Leavis, *New Bearings in English Poetry* (London: Chatto & Windus, 1932), p. 69.

12. Edna Longley, *Poetry in the Wars* (Newcastle: Bloodaxe Books, 1986), p. 55.

13. See above.

14. R. G. Thomas (ed.), *Edward Thomas: Selected Letters* (Oxford: Oxford University Press, 1995).

15. Anne Harvey (ed.), *Elected Friends (Poems for and about Edward Thomas)* (London: Enitharmon Press, 1991).

16. John Lehmann, 'Edward Thomas' in *The Open Night* (London: Longmans, 1952), p. 80.

17. Edward Thomas, Preface in *This England: An Anthology from her Writers* (London: Oxford University Press, 1915).
18. *Letters from Edward Thomas to Gordon Bottomley*, p. 155.

Edward Thomas

1914

Up in the Wind

'I could wring the old thing's neck that put it here!
A public house! it may be public for birds,
Squirrels, and such-like, ghosts of charcoal-burners
And highwaymen.' The wild girl laughed. 'But I
Hate it since I came back from Kennington.   5
I gave up a good place.' Her Cockney accent
Made her and the house seem wilder by calling up –
Only to be subdued at once by wildness –
The idea of London, there in that forest parlour,
Low and small among the towering beeches,   10
And the one bulging butt that's like a font.

Her eyes flashed up; she shook her hair away
From eyes and mouth, as if to shriek again;
Then sighed back to her scrubbing. While I drank
I might have mused of coaches and highwaymen,   15
Charcoal-burners and life that loves the wild.
For who now used these roads except myself,
A market waggon every other Wednesday,
A solitary tramp, some very fresh one
Ignorant of these eleven houseless miles,   20
A motorist from a distance slowing down
To taste whatever luxury he can
In having North Downs clear behind, South clear before,
And being midway between two railway lines,
Far out of sight or sound of them? There are   25
Some houses – down the by-lanes; and a few
Are visible – when their damsons are in bloom.
But the land is wild, and there's a spirit of wildness
Much older, crying when the stone-curlew yodels
His sea and mountain cry, high up in Spring.   30
He nests in fields where still the gorse is free as

When all was open and common. Common 'tis named
And calls itself, because the bracken and gorse
Still hold the hedge where plough and scythe have chased
    them.
Once on a time 'tis plain that 'The White Horse'   35
Stood merely on the border of waste
Where horse and cart picked its own course afresh.
On all sides then, as now, paths ran to the inn;
And now a farm-track takes you from a gate.

Two roads cross, and not a house in sight   40
Except 'The White Horse' in this clump of beeches.
It hides from either road, a field's breadth back;
And it's the trees you see, and not the house,
Both near and far, when the clump's the highest thing
And homely, too, upon a far horizon   45
To one that knows there is an inn within.

"Twould have been different,' the wild girl shrieked, 'suppose
That widow had married another blacksmith and
Kept on the business. This parlour was the smithy.
If she had done, there might never have been an inn;   50
And I, in that case, might never have been born.
Years ago, when this was all a wood
And the smith had charcoal-burners for company,
A man from a beech-country in the shires
Came with an engine and a little boy   55
(To feed the engine) to cut up timber here.
It all happened years ago. The smith
Had died, his widow had set up an alehouse –
I could wring the old thing's neck for thinking of it.
Well, I suppose they fell in love, the widow   60
And my great-uncle that sawed up the timber:
Leastways they married. The little boy stayed on.
He was my father.' She thought she'd scrub again –
'I draw the ale and he grows fat,' she muttered –
But only studied the hollows in the bricks   65
And chose among her thoughts in stirring silence.
The clock ticked, and the big saucepan lid
Heaved as the cabbage bubbled, and the girl

Questioned the fire and spoke: 'My father, he
Took to the land. A mile of it is worth   70
A guinea; for by that time all trees
Except these few about the house were gone:
That's all that's left of the forest unless you count
The bottoms of the charcoal-burners' fires –
We plough one up at times. Did you ever see   75
Our signboard?' No. The post and empty frame
I knew. Without them I should not have guessed
The low grey house and its one stack under trees
Was a public house and not a hermitage.
'But can that empty frame be any use?   80
Now I should like to see a good white horse,
Swing there, a really beautiful white horse,
Galloping one side, being painted on the other.'
'But would you like to hear it swing all night
And all day? All I ever had to thank   85
The wind for was for blowing the sign down.
Time after time it blew down and I could sleep.
At last they fixed it, and it took a thief
To move it, and we've never had another:
It's lying at the bottom of the pond.   90
But no one's moved the wood from off the hill
There at the back, although it makes a noise
When the wind blows, as if a train were running
The other side, a train that never stops
Or ends. And the linen crackles on the line   95
Like a wood fire rising.' 'But if you had the sign
You might draw company. What about Kennington?'
She bent down to her scrubbing with 'Not me:
Not back to Kennington. Here I was born,
And I've a notion on these windy nights   100
Here I shall die. Perhaps I want to die here.
I reckon I shall stay. But I do wish
The road was nearer and the wind farther off,
Or once now and then quite still, though when I die
I'd have it blowing that I might go with it   105
Somewhere distant, where there are trees no more
And I could wake and not know where I was
Nor even wonder if they would roar again.

Look at those calves.'

                              Between the open door
And the trees two calves were wading in the pond,   110
Grazing the water here and there and thinking,
Sipping and thinking, both happily, neither long.
The water wrinkled, but they sipped and thought,
As careless of the wind as it of us.
'Look at those calves. Hark at the trees again.'   115

November

November's days are thirty:
November's earth is dirty,
Those thirty days, from first to last;
And the prettiest things on ground are the paths
With morning and evening hobnails dinted,   5
With foot and wing-tip overprinted
Or separately charactered,
Of little beast and little bird.
The fields are mashed by sheep, the roads
Make the worst going, the best the woods   10
Where dead leaves upward and downward scatter.
Few care for the mixture of earth and water,
Twig, leaf, flint, thorn,
Straw, feather, all that men scorn,
Pounded up and sodden by flood,   15
Condemned as mud.

But of all the months when earth is greener
Not one has clean skies that are cleaner.
Clean and clear and sweet and cold,
They shine above the earth so old,   20
While the after-tempest cloud
Sails over in silence though winds are loud,
Till the full moon in the east

Looks at the planet in the west
And earth is silent as it is black,   25
Yet not unhappy for its lack.
Up from the dirty earth men stare:
One imagines a refuge there
Above the mud, in the pure bright
Of the cloudless heavenly light: 30
Another loves earth and November more dearly
Because without them, he sees clearly,
The sky would be nothing more to his eye
Than he, in any case, is to the sky;
He loves even the mud whose dyes   35
Renounce all brightness to the skies.

March

Now I know that Spring will come again,
Perhaps tomorrow: however late I've patience
After this night following on such a day.

While still my temples ached from the cold burning
Of hail and wind, and still the primroses   5
Torn by the hail were covered up in it,
The sun filled earth and heaven with a great light
And a tenderness, almost warmth, where the hail dripped,
As if the mighty sun wept tears of joy.
But 'twas too late for warmth. The sunset piled   10
Mountains on mountains of snow and ice in the west:
Somewhere among their folds the wind was lost,
And yet 'twas cold, and though I knew that Spring
Would come again, I knew it had not come,
That it was lost too in those mountains chill.   15

What did the thrushes know? Rain, snow, sleet, hail,
Had kept them quiet as the primroses.
They had but an hour to sing. On boughs they sang,

On gates, on ground; they sang while they changed perches
And while they fought, if they remembered to fight: 20
So earnest were they to pack into that hour
Their unwilling hoard of song before the moon
Grew brighter than the clouds. Then 'twas no time
For singing merely. So they could keep off silence
And night, they cared not what they sang or screamed;   25
Whether 'twas hoarse or sweet or fierce or soft;
And to me all was sweet: they could do no wrong.
Something they knew – I also, while they sang
And after. Not till night had half its stars
And never a cloud, was I aware of silence   30
Stained with all that hour's songs, a silence
Saying that Spring returns, perhaps tomorrow.

Old Man

Old Man, or Lad's-love, – in the name there's nothing
To one that knows not Lad's-love, or Old Man,
The hoar-green feathery herb, almost a tree,
Growing with rosemary and lavender.
Even to one that knows it well, the names   5
Half decorate, half perplex, the thing it is:
At least, what that is clings not to the names
In spite of time. And yet I like the names.

The herb itself I like not, but for certain
I love it, as some day the child will love it   10
Who plucks a feather from the door-side bush
Whenever she goes in or out of the house.
Often she waits there, snipping the tips and shrivelling
The shreds at last on to the path, perhaps
Thinking, perhaps of nothing, till she sniffs   15
Her fingers and runs off. The bush is still
But half as tall as she, though it is as old;
So well she clips it. Not a word she says;

And I can only wonder how much hereafter
She will remember, with that bitter scent,   20
Of garden rows, and ancient damson trees
Topping a hedge, a bent path to a door,
A low thick bush beside the door, and me
Forbidding her to pick.
                          As for myself,
Where first I met the bitter scent is lost.   25
I, too, often shrivel the grey shreds,
Sniff them and think and sniff again and try
Once more to think what it is I am remembering,
Always in vain. I cannot like the scent,
Yet I would rather give up others more sweet,   30
With no meaning, than this bitter one.

I have mislaid the key. I sniff the spray
And think of nothing; I see and I hear nothing;
Yet seem, too, to be listening, lying in wait
For what I should, yet never can, remember: 35
No garden appears, no path, no hoar-green bush
Of Lad's-love, or Old Man, no child beside,
Neither father nor mother, nor any playmate;
Only an avenue, dark, nameless, without end.

The Sign-Post

The dim sea glints chill. The white sun is shy,
And the skeleton weeds and the never-dry,
Rough, long grasses keep white with frost
At the hilltop by the finger-post;
The smoke of the traveller's-joy is puffed   5
Over hawthorn berry and hazel tuft.
I read the sign. Which way shall I go?
A voice says: You would not have doubted so
At twenty. Another voice gentle with scorn
Says: At twenty you wished you had never been born.   10

One hazel lost a leaf of gold
From a tuft at the tip, when the first voice told
The other he wished to know what 'twould be
To be sixty by this same post. 'You shall see,'
He laughed – and I had to join his laughter –   15
'You shall see; but either before or after,
Whatever happens, it must befall,
A mouthful of earth to remedy all
Regrets and wishes shall freely be given;
And if there be a flaw in that heaven   20
'Twill be freedom to wish, and your wish may be
To be here or anywhere talking to me,
No matter what the weather, on earth,
At any age between death and birth, –
To see what day or night can be,   25
The sun and the frost, the land and the sea,
Summer, Autumn, Winter, Spring, –
With a poor man of any sort, down to a king,
Standing upright out in the air
Wondering where he shall journey, O where?'   30

The Other

The forest ended. Glad I was
To feel the light, and hear the hum
Of bees, and smell the drying grass
And the sweet mint, because I had come
To an end of forest, and because   5
Here was both road and inn, the sum
Of what's not forest. But 'twas here
They asked me if I did not pass
Yesterday this way. 'Not you? Queer.'
'Who then? and slept here?' I felt fear.   10

I learnt his road and, ere they were
Sure I was I, left the dark wood

Behind, kestrel and woodpecker,
The inn in the sun, the happy mood
When first I tasted sunlight there.   15
I travelled fast, in hopes I should
Outrun that other. What to do
When caught, I planned not. I pursued
To prove the likeness, and, if true,
To watch until myself I knew.   20

I tried the inns that evening
Of a long gabled high-street grey,
Of courts and outskirts, travelling
An eager but a weary way,
In vain. He was not there. Nothing   25
Told me that ever till that day
Had one like me entered those doors,
Save once. That time I dared: 'You may
Recall' – but never-foamless shores
Make better friends than those dull boors.   30

Many and many a day like this
Aimed at the unseen moving goal
And nothing found but remedies
For all desire. These made not whole;
They sowed a new desire, to kiss   35
Desire's self beyond control,
Desire of desire. And yet
Life stayed on within my soul.
One night in sheltering from the wet
I quite forgot I could forget.   40

A customer, then the landlady
Stared at me. With a kind of smile
They hesitated awkwardly:
Their silence gave me time for guile.
Had anyone called there like me,   45
I asked. It was quite plain the wile
Succeeded. For they poured out all.
And that was naught. Less than a mile

Beyond the inn, I could recall
He was like me in general.   50

He had pleased them, but I less.
I was more eager than before
To find him out and to confess,
To bore him and to let him bore.
I could not wait: children might guess   55
I had a purpose, something more
That made an answer indiscreet.
One girl's caution made me sore,
Too indignant even to greet
That other had we chanced to meet.   60

I sought then in solitude.
The wind had fallen with the night; as still
The roads lay as the ploughland rude,
Dark and naked, on the hill.
Had there been ever any feud   65
'Twixt earth and sky, a mighty will
Closed it: the crocketed dark trees,
A dark house, dark impossible
Cloud-towers, one star, one lamp, one peace
Held on an everlasting lease: 70

And all was earth's, or all was sky's;
No difference endured between
The two. A dog barked on a hidden rise;
A marshbird whistled high unseen;
The latest waking blackbird's cries   75
Perished upon the silence keen.
The last light filled a narrow firth
Among the clouds. I stood serene,
And with a solemn quiet mirth,
An old inhabitant of earth.   80

Once the name I gave to hours
Like this was melancholy, when
It was not happiness and powers
Coming like exiles home again,

And weaknesses quitting their bowers,   85
Smiled and enjoyed, far off from men,
Moments of everlastingness.
And fortunate my search was then
While what I sought, nevertheless,
That I was seeking, I did not guess.   90

That time was brief: once more at inn
And upon road I sought my man
Till once amid a tap-room's din
Loudly he asked for me, began
To speak, as if it had been a sin,   95
Of how I thought and dreamed and ran
After him thus, day after day:
He lived as one under a ban
For this: what had I got to say?
I said nothing. I slipped away.   100

And now I dare not follow after
Too close. I try to keep in sight,
Dreading his frown and worse his laughter.
I steal out of the wood to light;
I see the swift shoot from the rafter   105
By the inn door: ere I alight
I wait and hear the starlings wheeze
And nibble like ducks: I wait his flight.
He goes: I follow: no release
Until he ceases. Then I also shall cease.   110

Interval

Gone the wild day:
A wilder night
Coming makes way
For brief twilight.

Where the firm soaked road   5
Mounts and is lost

In the high beech-wood
It shines almost.

The beeches keep
A stormy rest,   10
Breathing deep
Of wind from the west.

The wood is black,
With a misty steam.
Above, the cloud pack   15
Breaks for one gleam.

But the woodman's cot
By the ivied trees
Awakens not
To light or breeze.   20

It smokes aloft
Unwavering:
It hunches soft
Under storm's wing.

It has no care   25
For gleam or gloom:
It stays there
While I shall roam,

Die, and forget
The hill of trees,   30
The gleam, the wet,
This roaring peace.

Birds' Nests

The summer nests uncovered by autumn wind,
Some torn, others dislodged, all dark,
Everyone sees them: low or high in tree,
Or hedge, or single bush, they hang like a mark.

Since there's no need of eyes to see them with   5
I cannot help a little shame
That I missed most, even at eye's level, till
The leaves blew off and made the seeing no game.

'Tis a light pang. I like to see the nests
Still in their places, now first known,   10
At home and by far roads. Boys knew them not,
Whatever jays and squirrels may have done.

And most I like the winter nests deep-hid
That leaves and berries fell into:
Once a dormouse dined there on hazel-nuts,   15
And grass and goose-grass seeds found soil and grew.

The Mountain Chapel

Chapel and gravestones, old and few,
Are shrouded by a mountain fold
From sound and view
Of life. The loss of the brook's voice
Falls like a shadow. All they hear is   5
The eternal noise
Of wind whistling in grass more shrill
Than aught as human as a sword,
And saying still:
''Tis but a moment since man's birth   10
And in another moment more

Man lies in earth
For ever; but I am the same
Now, and shall be, even as I was
Before he came;   15
Till there is nothing I shall be.'
Yet there the sun shines after noon
So cheerfully
The place almost seems peopled, nor
Lacks cottage chimney, cottage hearth: 20
It is not more
In size than is a cottage, less
Than any other empty home
In homeliness.
It has a garden of wild flowers   25
And finest grass and gravestones warm
In sunshine hours
The year through. Men behind the glass
Stand once a week, singing, and drown
The whistling grass   30
Their ponies munch. And yet somewhere,
Near or far off, there's a man could
Live happy here,
Or one of the gods perhaps, were they
Not of inhuman stature dire,   35
As poets say
Who have not seen them clearly, if
At sound of any wind of the world
In grass-blades stiff
They would not startle and shudder cold   40
Under the sun. When gods were young
This wind was old.

The Manor Farm

The rock-like mud unfroze a little and rills
Ran and sparkled down each side of the road
Under the catkins wagging in the hedge.
But earth would have her sleep out, spite of the sun;
Nor did I value that thin gilding beam   5
More than a pretty February thing
Till I came down to the old Manor Farm,
And church and yew-tree opposite, in age
Its equals and in size. The church and yew
And farmhouse slept in a Sunday silentness.   10
The air raised not a straw. The steep farm roof,
With tiles duskily glowing, entertained
The mid-day sun; and up and down the roof
White pigeons nestled. There was no sound but one.
Three cart-horses were looking over a gate   15
Drowsily through their forelocks, swishing their tails
Against a fly, a solitary fly.

The Winter's cheek flushed as if he had drained
Spring, Summer, and Autumn at a draught
And smiled quietly. But 'twas not Winter –   20
Rather a season of bliss unchangeable
Awakened from farm and church where it had lain
Safe under tile and thatch for ages since
This England, Old already, was called Merry.

The Combe

The Combe was ever dark, ancient and dark.
Its mouth is stopped with bramble, thorn, and briar;
And no one scrambles over the sliding chalk
By beech and yew and perishing juniper
Down the half precipices of its sides, with roots   5

And rabbit holes for steps. The sun of Winter,
The moon of Summer, and all the singing birds
Except the missel-thrush that loves juniper,
Are quite shut out. But far more ancient and dark
The Combe looks since they killed the badger there,   10
Dug him out and gave him to the hounds,
That most ancient Briton of English beasts.

The Hollow Wood

Out in the sun the goldfinch flits
Along the thistle-tops, flits and twits
Above the hollow wood
Where birds swim like fish —
Fish that laugh and shriek —   5
To and fro, far below
In the pale hollow wood.

Lichen, ivy, and moss
Keep evergreen the trees
That stand half-flayed and dying,   10
And the dead trees on their knees
In dog's-mercury and moss:
And the bright twit of the goldfinch drops
Down there as he flits on thistle-tops.

1915

The New Year

He was the one man I met up in the woods
That stormy New Year's morning; and at first sight,
Fifty yards off, I could not tell how much
Of the strange tripod was a man. His body,
Bowed horizontal, was supported equally   5
By legs at one end, by a rake at the other:
Thus he rested, far less like a man than
His wheel-barrow in profile was like a pig.
But when I saw it was an old man bent,
At the same moment came into my mind   10
The games at which boys bend thus, *High-cocolorum*,
Or *Fly-the-garter*, and *Leap-frog*. At the sound
Of footsteps he began to straighten himself;
His head rolled under his cape like a tortoise's;
He took an unlit pipe out of his mouth   15
Politely ere I wished him 'A Happy New Year',
And with his head cast upward sideways muttered –
So far as I could hear through the trees' roar –
'Happy New Year, and may it come fastish, too,'
While I strode by and he turned to raking leaves.   20

The Penny Whistle

The new moon hangs like an ivory bugle
In the naked frosty blue;
And the ghylls of the forest, already blackened
By Winter, are blackened anew.

The brooks that cut up and increase the forest,   5
As if they had never known
The sun, are roaring with black hollow voices
Betwixt rage and a moan.

But still the caravan-hut by the hollies
Like a kingfisher gleams between: 10
Round the mossed old hearths of the charcoal-burners
First primroses ask to be seen.

The charcoal-burners are black, but their linen
Blows white on the line;
And white the letter the girl is reading   15
Under that crescent fine;

And her brother who hides apart in a thicket,
Slowly and surely playing
On a whistle an old nursery melody
Says far more than I am saying.   20

A Private

This ploughman dead in battle slept out of doors
Many a frozen night, and merrily
Answered staid drinkers, good bedmen, and all bores:
'At Mrs Greenland's Hawthorn Bush,' said he,
'I slept.' None knew which bush. Above the town,   5
Beyond 'The Drover', a hundred spot the down
In Wiltshire. And where now at last he sleeps
More sound in France – that, too, he secret keeps.

Snow

In the gloom of whiteness,
In the great silence of snow,
A child was sighing
And bitterly saying: 'Oh,
They have killed a white bird up there on her nest,   5
The down is fluttering from her breast!'
And still it fell through that dusky brightness
On the child crying for the bird of the snow.

Adlestrop

Yes. I remember Adlestrop –
The name, because one afternoon
Of heat the express-train drew up there
Unwontedly. It was late June.

The steam hissed. Someone cleared his throat.   5
No one left and no one came
On the bare platform. What I saw
Was Adlestrop – only the name

And willows, willow-herb, and grass,
And meadowsweet, and haycocks dry,   10
No whit less still and lonely fair
Than the high cloudlets in the sky.

And for that minute a blackbird sang
Close by, and round him, mistier,
Farther and farther, all the birds   15
Of Oxfordshire and Gloucestershire.

Tears

It seems I have no tears left. They should have fallen —
Their ghosts, if tears have ghosts, did fall — that day
When twenty hounds streamed by me, not yet combed out
But still all equals in their rage of gladness
Upon the scent, made one, like a great dragon   5
In Blooming Meadow that bends towards the sun
And once bore hops: and on that other day
When I stepped out from the double-shadowed Tower
Into an April morning, stirring and sweet
And warm. Strange solitude was there and silence.   10
A mightier charm than any in the Tower
Possessed the courtyard. They were changing guard,
Soldiers in line, young English countrymen,
Fair-haired and ruddy, in white tunics. Drums
And fifes were playing 'The British Grenadiers'.   15
The men, the music piercing that solitude
And silence, told me truths I had not dreamed,
And have forgotten since their beauty passed.

Over the Hills

Often and often it came back again
To mind, the day I passed the horizon ridge
To a new country, the path I had to find
By half-gaps that were stiles once in the hedge,
The pack of scarlet clouds running across   5
The harvest evening that seemed endless then
And after, and the inn where all were kind,
All were strangers. I did not know my loss
Till one day twelve months later suddenly
I leaned upon my spade and saw it all,   10
Though far beyond the sky-line. It became
Almost a habit through the year for me

To lean and see it and think to do the same
Again for two days and a night. Recall
Was vain: no more could the restless brook   15
Ever turn back and climb the waterfall
To the lake that rests and stirs not in its nook,
As in the hollow of the collar-bone
Under the mountain's head of rush and stone.

The Lofty Sky

Today I want the sky,
The tops of the high hills,
Above the last man's house,
His hedges, and his cows,
Where, if I will, I look   5
Down even on sheep and rook,
And of all things that move
See buzzards only above: –
Past all trees, past furze
And thorn, where nought deters   10
The desire of the eye
For sky, nothing but sky.
I sicken of the woods
And all the multitudes
Of hedge-trees. They are no more   15
Than weeds upon this floor
Of the river of air
Leagues deep, leagues wide, where
I am like a fish that lives
In weeds and mud and gives   20
What's above him no thought.
I might be a tench for aught
That I can do today
Down on the wealden clay.
Even the tench has days   25
When he floats up and plays

Among the lily leaves
And sees the sky, or grieves
Not if he nothing sees:
While I, I know that trees   30
Under that lofty sky
Are weeds, fields mud, and I
Would arise and go far
To where the lilies are.

Swedes

They have taken the gable from the roof of clay
On the long swede pile. They have let in the sun
To the white and gold and purple of curled fronds
Unsunned. It is a sight more tender-gorgeous
At the wood-corner where Winter moans and drips   5
Than when, in the Valley of the Tombs of Kings,
A boy crawls down into a Pharaoh's tomb
And, first of Christian men, beholds the mummy,
God and monkey, chariot and throne and vase,
Blue pottery, alabaster, and gold.   10

But dreamless long-dead Amen-hotep lies.
This is a dream of Winter, sweet as Spring.

The Unknown Bird

Three lovely notes he whistled, too soft to be heard
If others sang; but others never sang
In the great beech-wood all that May and June.
No one saw him: I alone could hear him

Though many listened. Was it but four years   5
Ago? or five? He never came again.

Oftenest when I heard him I was alone,
Nor could I ever make another hear.
La-la-la! he called, seeming far-off –
As if a cock crowed past the edge of the world,   10
As if the bird or I were in a dream.
Yet that he travelled through the trees and sometimes
Neared me, was plain, though somehow distant still
He sounded. All the proof is – I told men
What I had heard.

                          I never knew a voice,   15
Man, beast, or bird, better than this. I told
The naturalists; but neither had they heard
Anything like the notes that did so haunt me,
I had them clear by heart and have them still.
Four years, or five, have made no difference. Then   20
As now that La-la-la! was bodiless sweet:
Sad more than joyful it was, if I must say
That it was one or other, but if sad
'Twas sad only with joy too, too far off
For me to taste it. But I cannot tell   25
If truly never anything but fair
The days were when he sang, as now they seem.
This surely I know, that I who listened then,
Happy sometimes, sometimes suffering
A heavy body and a heavy heart,   30
Now straightway, if I think of it, become
Light as that bird wandering beyond my shore.

Man and Dog

''Twill take some getting.' 'Sir, I think 'twill so.
The old man stared up at the mistletoe
That hung too high in the poplar's crest for plunder
Of any climber, though not for kissing under:
Then he went on against the north-east wind –   5
Straight but lame, leaning on a staff new-skinned,
Carrying a brolly, flag-basket, and old coat, –
Towards Alton, ten miles off. And he had not
Done less from Chilgrove where he pulled up docks.
'Twere best, if he had had 'a money-box',   10
To have waited there till the sheep cleared a field
For what a half-week's flint-picking would yield.
His mind was running on the work he had done
Since he left Christchurch in the New Forest, one
Spring in the 'seventies, – navvying on dock and line   15
From Southampton to Newcastle-on-Tyne, –
In 'seventy-four a year of soldiering
With the Berkshires, – hoeing and harvesting
In half the shires where corn and couch will grow.
His sons, three sons, were fighting, but the hoe   20
And reap-hook he liked, or anything to do with trees.
He fell once from a poplar tall as these:
The Flying Man they called him in hospital.
'If I flew now, to another world I'd fall.'
He laughed and whistled to the small brown bitch   25
With spots of blue that hunted in the ditch.
Her foxy Welsh grandfather must have paired
Beneath him. He kept sheep in Wales and scared
Strangers, I will warrant, with his pearl eye
And trick of shrinking off as he were shy,   30
Then following close in silence for – for what?
'No rabbit, never fear, she ever got,
Yet always hunts. Today she nearly had one:
She would and she wouldn't. 'Twas like that. The bad one!
She's not much use, but still she's company,   35
Though I'm not. She goes everywhere with me.
So Alton I must reach tonight somehow:

I'll get no shakedown with that bedfellow
From farmers. Many a man sleeps worse tonight
Than I shall.' 'In the trenches.' 'Yes, that's right.   40
But they'll be out of that – I hope they be –
This weather, marching after the enemy.'
'And so I hope. Good luck.' And there I nodded
'Good-night. You keep straight on.' Stiffly he plodded;
And at his heels the crisp leaves scurried fast,   45
And the leaf-coloured robin watched. They passed,
The robin till next day, the man for good,
Together in the twilight of the wood.

Beauty

What does it mean? Tired, angry, and ill at ease,
No man, woman, or child alive could please
Me now. And yet I almost dare to laugh
Because I sit and frame an epitaph –
'Here lies all that no one loved of him   5
And that loved no one.' Then in a trice that whim
Has wearied. But, though I am like a river
At fall of evening while it seems that never
Has the sun lighted it or warmed it, while
Cross breezes cut the surface to a file,   10
This heart, some fraction of me, happily
Floats through the window even now to a tree
Down in the misting, dim-lit, quiet vale,
Not like a pewit that returns to wail
For something it has lost, but like a dove   15
That slants unswerving to its home and love.
There I find my rest, and through the dusk air
Flies what yet lives in me. Beauty is there.

The Gypsy

A fortnight before Christmas Gypsies were everywhere:
Vans were drawn up on wastes, women trailed to the fair.
'My gentleman,' said one, 'you've got a lucky face.'
'And you've a luckier,' I thought, 'if such a grace
And impudence in rags are lucky.' 'Give a penny   5
For the poor baby's sake.' 'Indeed I have not any
Unless you can give change for a sovereign, my dear.'
'Then just half a pipeful of tobacco can you spare?'
I gave it. With that much victory she laughed content.
I should have given more, but off and away she went   10
With her baby and her pink sham flowers to rejoin
The rest before I could translate to its proper coin
Gratitude for her grace. And I paid nothing then,
As I pay nothing now with the dipping of my pen
For her brother's music when he drummed the tambourine   15
And stamped his feet, which made the workmen passing grin,
While his mouth-organ changed to a rascally Bacchanal dance
'Over the hills and far away'. This and his glance
Outlasted all the fair, farmer, and auctioneer,
Cheap-jack, balloon-man, drover with crooked stick, and steer,   20
Pig, turkey, goose, and duck, Christmas corpses to be.
Not even the kneeling ox had eyes like the Romany.
That night he peopled for me the hollow wooded land,
More dark and wild than stormiest heavens, that I searched and
    scanned
Like a ghost new-arrived. The gradations of the dark   25
Were like an underworld of death, but for the spark
In the Gypsy boy's black eyes as he played and stamped his tune,
'Over the hills and far away', and a crescent moon.

Parting

The Past is a strange land, most strange.
Wind blows not there, nor does rain fall:
If they do, they cannot hurt at all.
Men of all kinds as equals range

The soundless fields and streets of it.   5
Pleasure and pain there have no sting,
The perished self not suffering
That lacks all blood and nerve and wit,

And is in shadow-land a shade.
Remembered joy and misery   10
Bring joy to the joyous equally;
Both sadden the sad. So memory made

Parting today a double pain:
First because it was parting; next
Because the ill it ended vexed   15
And mocked me from the Past again,

Not as what had been remedied
Had I gone on, – not that, oh no!
But as itself no longer woe;
Sighs, angry word and look and deed   20

Being faded: rather a kind of bliss,
For there spiritualized it lay
In the perpetual yesterday
That naught can stir or strain like this.

First Known when Lost

I never had noticed it until
'Twas gone, – the narrow copse
Where now the woodman lops
The last of the willows with his bill.

It was not more than a hedge overgrown.   5
One meadow's breadth away
I passed it day by day.
Now the soil is bare as a bone,

And black betwixt two meadows green,
Though fresh-cut faggot ends   10
Of hazel made some amends
With a gleam as if flowers they had been.

Strange it could have hidden so near!
And now I see as I look
That the small winding brook,   15
A tributary's tributary, rises there.

May the Twenty-third

There never was a finer day,
And never will be while May is May, –
The third, and not the last of its kind;
But though fair and clear the two behind
Seemed pursued by tempests overpast;   5
And the morrow with fear that it could not last
Was spoiled. Today ere the stones were warm
Five minutes of thunderstorm
Dashed it with rain, as if to secure,
By one tear, its beauty the luck to endure.   10

At midday then along the lane
Old Jack Noman appeared again,
Jaunty and old, crooked and tall,
And stopped and grinned at me over the wall,
With a cowslip bunch in his button-hole   15
And one in his cap. Who could say if his roll
Came from flints in the road, the weather, or ale?
He was welcome as the nightingale.
Not an hour of the sun had been wasted on Jack.
'I've got my Indian complexion back,'   20
Said he. He was tanned like a harvester,
Like his short clay pipe, like the leaf and bur
That clung to his coat from last night's bed,
Like the ploughland crumbling red.
Fairer flowers were none on the earth   25
Than his cowslips wet with the dew of their birth,
Or fresher leaves than the cress in his basket.
'Where did they come from, Jack?' 'Don't ask it,
And you'll be told no lies.' 'Very well:
Then I can't buy.' 'I don't want to sell.   30
Take them and these flowers, too, free.
Perhaps you have something to give me?
Wait till next time. The better the day . . .
The Lord couldn't make a better, I say;
If he could, he never has done.'   35
So off went Jack with his roll-walk-run,
Leaving his cresses from Oakshott rill
And his cowslips from Wheatham hill.

'Twas the first day that the midges bit;
But though they bit me, I was glad of it: 40
Of the dust in my face, too, I was glad.
Spring could do nothing to make me sad.
Bluebells hid all the ruts in the copse,
The elm seeds lay in the road like hops,
That fine day, May the twenty-third,   45
The day Jack Noman disappeared.

The Barn

They should never have built a barn there, at all –
Drip, drip, drip! – under that elm tree,
Though then it was young. Now it is old
But good, not like the barn and me.

Tomorrow they cut it down. They will leave   5
The barn, as I shall be left, maybe.
What holds it up? 'Twould not pay to pull down.
Well, this place has no other antiquity.

No abbey or castle looks so old
As this that Job Knight built in '54,   10
Built to keep corn for rats and men.
Now there's fowls in the roof, pigs on the floor.

What thatch survives is dung for the grass,
The best grass on the farm. A pity the roof
Will not bear a mower to mow it. But   15
Only fowls have foothold enough.

Starlings used to sit there with bubbling throats
Making a spiky beard as they chattered
And whistled and kissed, with heads in air,
Till they thought of something else that mattered.   20

But now they cannot find a place,
Among all those holes, for a nest any more.
It's the turn of lesser things, I suppose.
Once I fancied 'twas starlings they built it for.

Home [1]

Not the end: but there's nothing more.
Sweet Summer and Winter rude
I have loved, and friendship and love,
The crowd and solitude:

But I know them: I weary not;   5
But all that they mean I know.
I would go back again home
Now. Yet how should I go?

This is my grief. That land,
My home, I have never seen;   10
No traveller tells of it,
However far he has been.

And could I discover it,
I fear my happiness there,
Or my pain, might be dreams of return   15
Here, to these things that were.

Remembering ills, though slight
Yet irremediable,
Brings a worse, an impurer pang
Than remembering what was well.   20

No: I cannot go back,
And would not if I could.
Until blindness come, I must wait
And blink at what is not good.

The Owl

Downhill I came, hungry, and yet not starved;
Cold, yet had heat within me that was proof
Against the North wind; tired, yet so that rest
Had seemed the sweetest thing under a roof.

Then at the inn I had food, fire, and rest,   5
Knowing how hungry, cold, and tired was I.
All of the night was quite barred out except
An owl's cry, a most melancholy cry

Shaken out long and clear upon the hill,
No merry note, nor cause of merriment,   10
But one telling me plain what I escaped
And others could not, that night, as in I went.

And salted was my food, and my repose,
Salted and sobered, too, by the bird's voice
Speaking for all who lay under the stars,   15
Soldiers and poor, unable to rejoice.

The Bridge

I have come a long way today:
On a strange bridge alone,
Remembering friends, old friends,
I rest, without smile or moan,
As they remember me without smile or moan.   5

All are behind, the kind
And the unkind too, no more
Tonight than a dream. The stream
Runs softly yet drowns the Past,
The dark-lit stream has drowned the Future and the Past.   10

No traveller has rest more blest
Than this moment brief between
Two lives, when the Night's first lights
And shades hide what has never been,
Things goodlier, lovelier, dearer, than will be or have been.   15

But These Things Also

But these things also are Spring's –
On banks by the roadside the grass
Long-dead that is greyer now
Than all the Winter it was;

The shell of a little snail bleached   5
In the grass; chip of flint, and mite
Of chalk; and the small birds' dung
In splashes of purest white:

All the white things a man mistakes
For earliest violets   10
Who seeks through Winter's ruins
Something to pay Winter's debts,

While the North blows, and starling flocks
By chattering on and on
Keep their spirits up in the mist,   15
And Spring's here, Winter's not gone.

The New House

Now first, as I shut the door,
   I was alone
In the new house; and the wind
   Began to moan.

Old at once was the house,   5
   And I was old;
My ears were teased with the dread
   Of what was foretold,

Nights of storm, days of mist, without end;
   Sad days when the sun   10
Shone in vain: old griefs and griefs
   Not yet begun.

All was foretold me; naught
   Could I foresee;
But I learned how the wind would sound   15
   After these things should be.

Sowing

It was a perfect day
For sowing; just
As sweet and dry was the ground
As tobacco-dust.

I tasted deep the hour   5
Between the far
Owl's chuckling first soft cry
And the first star.

A long stretched hour it was;
Nothing undone   10
Remained; the early seeds
All safely sown.

And now, hark at the rain,
Windless and light,
Half a kiss, half a tear,   15
Saying good-night.

Two Pewits

Under the after-sunset sky
Two pewits sport and cry,
More white than is the moon on high
Riding the dark surge silently;
More black than earth. Their cry   5
Is the one sound under the sky.
They alone move, now low, now high,
And merrily they cry
To the mischievous Spring sky,
Plunging earthward, tossing high,   10
Over the ghost who wonders why
So merrily they cry and fly,
Nor choose 'twixt earth and sky,
While the moon's quarter silently
Rides, and earth rests as silently.   15

The Path

Running along a bank, a parapet
That saves from the precipitous wood below
The level road, there is a path. It serves
Children for looking down the long smooth steep,
Between the legs of beech and yew, to where   5
A fallen tree checks the sight: while men and women
Content themselves with the road and what they see
Over the bank, and what the children tell.
The path, winding like silver, trickles on,
Bordered and even invaded by thinnest moss   10
That tries to cover roots and crumbling chalk
With gold, olive, and emerald, but in vain.
The children wear it. They have flattened the bank
On top, and silvered it between the moss
With the current of their feet, year after year.   15
But the road is houseless, and leads not to school.
To see a child is rare there, and the eye
Has but the road, the wood that overhangs
And underyawns it, and the path that looks
As if it led on to some legendary   20
Or fancied place where men have wished to go
And stay; till, sudden, it ends where the wood ends.

A Tale

There once the walls
Of the ruined cottage stood.
The periwinkle crawls
With flowers in its hair into the wood.

In flowerless hours   5
Never will the bank fail,
With everlasting flowers
On fragments of blue plates, to tell the tale.

Wind and Mist

They met inside the gateway that gives the view,
A hollow land as vast as heaven. 'It is
A pleasant day, sir.' 'A very pleasant day.'
'And what a view here! If you like angled fields
Of grass and grain bounded by oak and thorn,   5
Here is a league. Had we with Germany
To play upon this board it could not be
More dear than April has made it with a smile.
The fields beyond that league close in together
And merge, even as our days into the past,   10
Into one wood that has a shining pane
Of water. Then the hills of the horizon –
That is how I should make hills had I to show
One who would never see them what hills were like.'
'Yes. Sixty miles of South Downs at one glance.   15
Sometimes a man feels proud of them, as if
He had just created them with one mighty thought.'
'That house, though modern, could not be better planned
For its position. I never liked a new
House better. Could you tell me who lives in it?'   20
'No one.' 'Ah – and I was peopling all
Those windows on the south with happy eyes,
The terrace under them with happy feet;
Girls –' 'Sir, I know. I know. I have seen that house
Through mist look lovely as a castle in Spain,   25
And airier. I have thought: '"Twere happy there
To live." And I have laughed at that
Because I lived there then.' 'Extraordinary.'
'Yes, with my furniture and family
Still in it, I, knowing every nook of it   30
And loving none, and in fact hating it.'
'Dear me! How could that be? But pardon me.'
'No offence. Doubtless the house was not to blame,
But the eye watching from those windows saw,
Many a day, day after day, mist – mist   35
Like chaos surging back – and felt itself
Alone in all the world, marooned alone.

We lived in clouds, on a cliff's edge almost
(You see), and if clouds went, the visible earth
Lay too far off beneath and like a cloud.   40
I did not know it was the earth I loved
Until I tried to live there in the clouds
And the earth turned to cloud.' 'You had a garden
Of flint and clay, too.' 'True; that was real enough.
The flint was the one crop that never failed.   45
The clay first broke my heart, and then my back;
And the back heals not. There were other things
Real, too. In that room at the gable a child
Was born while the wind chilled a summer dawn:
Never looked grey mind on a greyer one   50
Than when the child's cry broke above the groans.'
'I hope they were both spared.' 'They were. Oh yes!
But flint and clay and childbirth were too real
For this cloud-castle. I had forgot the wind.
Pray do not let me get on to the wind.   55
You would not understand about the wind.
It is my subject, and compared with me
Those who have always lived on the firm ground
Are quite unreal in this matter of the wind.
There were whole days and nights when the wind and I   60
Between us shared the world, and the wind ruled
And I obeyed it and forgot the mist.
My past and the past of the world were in the wind.
Now you may say that though you understand
And feel for me, and so on, you yourself   65
Would find it different. You are all like that
If once you stand here free from wind and mist:
I might as well be talking to wind and mist.
You would believe the house-agent's young man
Who gives no heed to anything I say.   70
Good-morning. But one word. I want to admit
That I would try the house once more, if I could;
As I should like to try being young again.'

Lob

At hawthorn-time in Wiltshire travelling
In search of something chance would never bring,
An old man's face, by life and weather cut
And coloured, – rough, brown, sweet as any nut, –
A land face, sea-blue-eyed, – hung in my mind   5
When I had left him many a mile behind.
All he said was: 'Nobody can't stop 'ee. It's
A footpath, right enough. You see those bits
Of mounds – that's where they opened up the barrows
Sixty years since, while I was scaring sparrows.   10
They thought as there was something to find there,
But couldn't find it, by digging, anywhere.'

To turn back then and seek him, where was the use?
There were three Manningfords, – Abbots, Bohun, and Bruce:
And whether Alton, not Manningford, it was,   15
My memory could not decide, because
There was both Alton Barnes and Alton Priors.
All had their churches, graveyards, farms, and byres,
Lurking to one side up the paths and lanes,
Seldom well seen except by aeroplanes;   20
And when bells rang, or pigs squealed, or cocks crowed,
Then only heard. Ages ago the road
Approached. The people stood and looked and turned.
Nor asked it to come nearer, nor yet learned
To move out there and dwell in all men's dust.   25
And yet withal they shot the weathercock, just
Because 'twas he crowed out of tune, they said:
So now the copper weathercock is dead.
If they had reaped their dandelions and sold
Them fairly, they could have afforded gold.   30

Many years passed, and I went back again
Among those villages, and looked for men
Who might have known my ancient. He himself
Had long been dead or laid upon the shelf,
I thought. One man I asked about him roared   35

At my description: ''Tis old Bottlesford
He means, Bill.' But another said: 'Of course,
It was Jack Button up at the White Horse.
He's dead, sir, these three years.' This lasted till
A girl proposed Walker of Walker's Hill,   40
'Old Adam Walker. Adam's Point you'll see
Marked on the maps.'

                              'That was her roguery,'
The next man said. He was a squire's son
Who loved wild bird and beast, and dog and gun
For killing them. He had loved them from his birth,   45
One with another, as he loved the earth.
'The man may be like Button, or Walker, or
Like Bottlesford, that you want, but far more
He sounds like one I saw when I was a child.
I could almost swear to him. The man was wild   50
And wandered. His home was where he was free.
Everybody has met one such man as he.
Does he keep clear old paths that no one uses
But once a lifetime when he loves or muses?
He is English as this gate, these flowers, this mire.   55
And when at eight years old Lob-lie-by-the-fire
Came in my books, this was the man I saw.
He has been in England as long as dove and daw,
Calling the wild cherry tree the merry tree,
The rose campion Bridget-in-her-bravery;   60
And in a tender mood he, as I guess,
Christened one flower Love-in-idleness,
And while he walked from Exeter to Leeds
One April called all cuckoo-flowers Milkmaids.
From him old herbal Gerard learnt, as a boy,   65
To name wild clematis the Traveller's-joy.
Our blackbirds sang no English till his ear
Told him they called his Jan Toy ''Pretty dear''.
(She was Jan Toy the Lucky, who, having lost
A shilling, and found a penny loaf, rejoiced.)   70
For reasons of his own to him the wren
Is Jenny Pooter. Before all other men
'Twas he first called the Hog's Back the Hog's Back.

That Mother Dunch's Buttocks should not lack
Their name was his care. He too could explain   75
Totteridge and Totterdown and Juggler's Lane:
He knows, if anyone. Why Tumbling Bay,
Inland in Kent, is called so, he might say.

'But little he says compared with what he does.
If ever a sage troubles him he will buzz   80
Like a beehive to conclude the tedious fray:
And the sage, who knows all languages, runs away.
Yet Lob has thirteen hundred names for a fool,
And though he never could spare time for school
To unteach what the fox so well expressed,   85
On biting the cock's head off, – Quietness is best, –
He can talk quite as well as anyone
After his thinking is forgot and done.
He first of all told someone else's wife,
For a farthing she'd skin a flint and spoil a knife   90
Worth sixpence skinning it. She heard him speak:
"She had a face as long as a wet week"
Said he, telling the tale in after years.
With blue smock and with gold rings in his ears,
Sometimes he is a pedlar, not too poor   95
To keep his wit. This is tall Tom that bore
The logs in, and with Shakespeare in the hall
Once talked, when icicles hung by the wall.
As Herne the Hunter he has known hard times.
On sleepless nights he made up weather rhymes   100
Which others spoilt. And, Hob being then his name,
He kept the hog that thought the butcher came
To bring his breakfast. "You thought wrong", said Hob.
When there were kings in Kent this very Lob,
Whose sheep grew fat and he himself grew merry,   105
Wedded the king's daughter of Canterbury;
For he alone, unlike squire, lord, and king,
Watched a night by her without slumbering;
He kept both waking. When he was but a lad
He won a rich man's heiress, deaf, dumb, and sad,   110
By rousing her to laugh at him. He carried
His donkey on his back. So they were married.

And while he was a little cobbler's boy
He tricked the giant coming to destroy
Shrewsbury by flood. "And how far is it yet?"   115
The giant asked in passing. "I forget;
But see these shoes I've worn out on the road
And we're not there yet." He emptied out his load
Of shoes for mending. The giant let fall from his spade
The earth for damming Severn, and thus made   120
The Wrekin hill; and little Ercall hill
Rose where the giant scraped his boots. While still
So young, our Jack was chief of Gotham's sages.
But long before he could have been wise, ages
Earlier than this, while he grew thick and strong   125
And ate his bacon, or, at times, sang a song
And merely smelt it, as Jack the giant-killer
He made a name. He too ground up the miller,
The Yorkshireman who ground men's bones for flour.

'Do you believe Jack dead before his hour?   130
Or that his name is Walker, or Bottlesford,
Or Button, a mere clown, or squire, or lord?
The man you saw, – Lob-lie-by-the-fire, Jack Cade,
Jack Smith, Jack Moon, poor Jack of every trade,
Young Jack, or old Jack, or Jack What-d'ye-call,   135
Jack-in-the-hedge, or Robin-run-by-the-wall,
Robin Hood, Ragged Robin, lazy Bob,
One of the lords of No Man's Land, good Lob, –
Although he was seen dying at Waterloo,
Hastings, Agincourt, and Sedgemoor too, –   140
Lives yet. He never will admit he is dead
Till millers cease to grind men's bones for bread,
Not till our weathercock crows once again
And I remove my house out of the lane
On to the road.' With this he disappeared   145
In hazel and thorn tangled with old-man's-beard.
But one glimpse of his back, as there he stood,
Choosing his way, proved him of old Jack's blood,
Young Jack perhaps, and now a Wiltshireman
As he has oft been since his days began.   150

Digging [1]

Today I think
Only with scents, – scents dead leaves yield,
And bracken, and wild carrot's seed,
And the square mustard field;

Odours that rise   5
When the spade wounds the root of tree,
Rose, currant, raspberry, or goutweed,
Rhubarb or celery;

The smoke's smell, too,
Flowing from where a bonfire burns   10
The dead, the waste, the dangerous,
And all to sweetness turns.

It is enough
To smell, to crumble the dark earth,
While the robin sings over again   15
Sad songs of Autumn mirth.

Lovers

The two men in the road were taken aback.
The lovers came out shading their eyes from the sun,
And never was white so white, or black so black,
As her cheeks and hair. 'There are more things than one
A man might turn into a wood for, Jack,'   5
Said George; Jack whispered: 'He has not got a gun.
It's a bit too much of a good thing, I say.
They are going the other road, look. And see her run.' –
She ran. – 'What a thing it is, this picking may!'

In Memoriam (Easter, 1915)

The flowers left thick at nightfall in the wood
This Eastertide call into mind the men,
Now far from home, who, with their sweethearts, should
Have gathered them and will do never again.

Head and Bottle

The downs will lose the sun, white alyssum
Lose the bees' hum;
But head and bottle tilted back in the cart
Will never part
Till I am cold as midnight and all my hours   5
Are beeless flowers.
He neither sees, nor hears, nor smells, nor thinks,
But only drinks,
Quiet in the yard where tree trunks do not lie
More quietly.   10

Home [2]

Often I had gone this way before:
But now it seemed I never could be
And never had been anywhere else;
'Twas home; one nationality
We had, I and the birds that sang,   5
One memory.

They welcomed me. I had come back
That eve somehow from somewhere far:

The April mist, the chill, the calm,
Meant the same thing familiar   10
And pleasant to us, and strange too,
Yet with no bar.

The thrush on the oaktop in the lane
Sang his last song, or last but one;
And as he ended, on the elm   15
Another had but just begun
His last; they knew no more than I
The day was done.

Then past his dark white cottage front
A labourer went along, his tread   20
Slow, half with weariness, half with ease;
And, through the silence, from his shed
The sound of sawing rounded all
That silence said.

Health

Four miles at a leap, over the dark hollow land,
To the frosted steep of the down and its junipers black,
Travels my eye with equal ease and delight:
And scarce could my body leap four yards.

This is the best and the worst of it –   5
Never to know,
Yet to imagine gloriously, pure health.

Today, had I suddenly health,
I could not satisfy the desire of my heart
Unless health abated it,   10
So beautiful is the air in its softness and clearness, while Spring
Promises all and fails in nothing as yet;

And what blue and what white is I never knew
Before I saw this sky blessing the land.

For had I health I could not ride or run or fly   15
So far or so rapidly over the land
As I desire: I should reach Wiltshire tired;
I should have changed my mind before I could be in Wales.
I could not love; I could not command love.
Beauty would still be far off   20
However many hills I climbed over;
Peace would still be farther.
Maybe I should not count it anything
To leap these four miles with the eye;
And either I should not be filled almost to bursting with desire,   25
Or with my power desire would still keep pace.

Yet I am not satisfied
Even with knowing I never could be satisfied.
With health and all the power that lies
In maiden beauty, poet and warrior,   30
In Caesar, Shakespeare, Alcibiades,
Mazeppa, Leonardo, Michelangelo,
In any maiden whose smile is lovelier
Than sunlight upon dew,
I could not be as the wagtail running up and down   35
The warm tiles of the roof slope, twittering
Happily and sweetly as if the sun itself
Extracted the song
As the hand makes sparks from the fur of a cat:

I could not be as the sun.   40
Nor should I be content to be
As little as the bird or as mighty as the sun.
For the bird knows not of the sun,
And the sun regards not the bird.
But I am almost proud to love both bird and sun,   45
Though scarce this Spring could my body leap four yards.

Melancholy

The rain and wind, the rain and wind, raved endlessly.
On me the Summer storm, and fever, and melancholy
Wrought magic, so that if I feared the solitude
Far more I feared all company: too sharp, too rude,
Had been the wisest or the dearest human voice. 5
What I desired I knew not, but whate'er my choice
Vain it must be, I knew. Yet naught did my despair
But sweeten the strange sweetness, while through the wild air
All day long I heard a distant cuckoo calling
And, soft as dulcimers, sounds of near water falling, 10
And, softer, and remote as if in history,
Rumours of what had touched my friends, my foes, or me.

The Glory

The glory of the beauty of the morning, —
The cuckoo crying over the untouched dew;
The blackbird that has found it, and the dove
That tempts me on to something sweeter than love;
White clouds ranged even and fair as new-mown hay; 5
The heat, the stir, the sublime vacancy
Of sky and meadow and forest and my own heart: —
The glory invites me, yet it leaves me scorning
All I can ever do, all I can be,
Beside the lovely of motion, shape, and hue, 10
The happiness I fancy fit to dwell
In beauty's presence. Shall I now this day
Begin to seek as far as heaven, as hell,
Wisdom or strength to match this beauty, start
And tread the pale dust pitted with small dark drops, 15
In hope to find whatever it is I seek,
Hearkening to short-lived happy-seeming things

That we know naught of, in the hazel copse?
Or must I be content with discontent
As larks and swallows are perhaps with wings?   20
And shall I ask at the day's end once more
What beauty is, and what I can have meant
By happiness? And shall I let all go,
Glad, weary, or both? Or shall I perhaps know
That I was happy oft and oft before,   25
Awhile forgetting how I am fast pent,
How dreary-swift, with naught to travel to,
Is Time? I cannot bite the day to the core.

July

Naught moves but clouds, and in the glassy lake
Their doubles and the shadow of my boat.
The boat itself stirs only when I break
This drowse of heat and solitude afloat
To prove if what I see be bird or mote,   5
Or learn if yet the shore woods be awake.

Long hours since dawn grew, – spread, – and passed on high
And deep below, – I have watched the cool reeds hung
Over images more cool in imaged sky:
Nothing there was worth thinking of so long;   10
All that the ring-doves say, far leaves among,
Brims my mind with content thus still to lie.

The Chalk-Pit

'Is this the road that climbs above and bends
Round what was once a chalk-pit: now it is
By accident an amphitheatre.
Some ash trees standing ankle-deep in briar
And bramble act the parts, and neither speak   5
Nor stir.' 'But see: they have fallen, every one,
And briar and bramble have grown over them.'
'That is the place. As usual no one is here.
Hardly can I imagine the drop of the axe,
And the smack that is like an echo, sounding here.'   10
'I do not understand.' 'Why, what I mean is
That I have seen the place two or three times
At most, and that its emptiness and silence
And stillness haunt me, as if just before
It was not empty, silent, still, but full   15
Of life of some kind, perhaps tragical.
Has anything unusual happened here?'
'Not that I know of. It is called the Dell.
They have not dug chalk here for a century.
That was the ash trees' age. But I will ask.'   20
'No. Do not. I prefer to make a tale,
Or better leave it like the end of a play,
Actors and audience and lights all gone;
For so it looks now. In my memory
Again and again I see it, strangely dark,   25
And vacant of a life but just withdrawn.
We have not seen the woodman with the axe.
Some ghost has left it now as we two came.'
'And yet you doubted if this were the road?'
'Well, sometimes I have thought of it and failed   30
To place it. No. And I am not quite sure,
Even now, this is it. For another place,
Real or painted, may have combined with it.
Or I myself a long way back in time . . .'
'Why, as to that, I used to meet a man –   35
I had forgotten, – searching for birds' nests
Along the road and in the chalk-pit too.

The wren's hole was an eye that looked at him
For recognition. Every nest he knew.
He got a stiff neck, by looking this side or that,   40
Spring after spring, he told me, with his laugh, –
A sort of laugh. He was a visitor,
A man of forty, – smoked and strolled about.
At orts and crosses Pleasure and Pain had played
On his brown features; – I think both had lost; –   45
Mild and yet wild too. You may know the kind.
And once or twice a woman shared his walks,
A girl of twenty with a brown boy's face,
And hair brown as a thrush or as a nut,
Thick eyebrows, glinting eyes –' 'You have said enough.   50
A pair, – free thought, free love, – I know the breed:
I shall not mix my fancies up with them.'
'You please yourself. I should prefer the truth
Or nothing. Here, in fact, is nothing at all
Except a silent place that once rang loud,   55
And trees and us – imperfect friends, we men
And trees since time began; and nevertheless
Between us still we breed a mystery.'

Fifty Faggots

There they stand, on their ends, the fifty faggots
That once were underwood of hazel and ash
In Jenny Pinks's Copse. Now, by the hedge
Close packed, they make a thicket fancy alone
Can creep through with the mouse and wren. Next Spring   5
A blackbird or a robin will nest there,
Accustomed to them, thinking they will remain
Whatever is for ever to a bird:
This Spring it is too late; the swift has come.
'Twas a hot day for carrying them up: 10
Better they will never warm me, though they must
Light several Winters' fires. Before they are done

The war will have ended, many other things
Have ended, maybe, that I can no more
Foresee or more control than robin and wren.   15

Sedge-Warblers

This beauty made me dream there was a time
Long past and irrecoverable, a clime
Where any brook so radiant racing clear
Through buttercup and kingcup bright as brass
But gentle, nourishing the meadow grass   5
That leans and scurries in the wind, would bear
Another beauty, divine and feminine,
Child to the sun, a nymph whose soul unstained
Could love all day, and never hate or tire,
A lover of mortal or immortal kin.   10

And yet, rid of this dream, ere I had drained
Its poison, quieted was my desire
So that I only looked into the water,
Clearer than any goddess or man's daughter,
And hearkened while it combed the dark green hair   15
And shook the millions of the blossoms white
Of water-crowfoot, and curdled to one sheet
The flowers fallen from the chestnuts in the park
Far off. And sedge-warblers, clinging so light
To willow twigs, sang longer than the lark,   20
Quick, shrill, or grating, a song to match the heat
Of the strong sun, nor less the water's cool,
Gushing through narrows, swirling in the pool.
Their song that lacks all words, all melody,
All sweetness almost, was dearer then to me   25
Than sweetest voice that sings in tune sweet words.
This was the best of May – the small brown birds
Wisely reiterating endlessly
What no man learnt yet, in or out of school.

I Built Myself a House of Glass

I built myself a house of glass:
It took me years to make it:
And I was proud. But now, alas!
Would God someone would break it.

But it looks too magnificent.   5
No neighbour casts a stone
From where he dwells, in tenement
Or palace of glass, alone.

Words

Out of us all
That make rhymes,
Will you choose
Sometimes –
As the winds use   5
A crack in a wall
Or a drain,
Their joy or their pain
To whistle through –
Choose me,   10
You English words?

I know you:
You are light as dreams,
Tough as oak,
Precious as gold,   15
As poppies and corn,
Or an old cloak:
Sweet as our birds
To the ear,
As the burnet rose   20

In the heat
Of Midsummer:
Strange as the races
Of dead and unborn:
Strange and sweet   25
Equally,
And familiar,
To the eye,
As the dearest faces
That a man knows,   30
And as lost homes are:
But though older far
Than oldest yew, –
As our hills are, old, –
Worn new   35
Again and again:
Young as our streams
After rain:
And as dear
As the earth which you prove   40
That we love.

Make me content
With some sweetness
From Wales
Whose nightingales   45
Have no wings, –
From Wiltshire and Kent
And Herefordshire,
And the villages there, –
From the names, and the things   50
No less.
Let me sometimes dance
With you,
Or climb
Or stand perchance   55
In ecstasy,
Fixed and free
In a rhyme,
As poets do.

The Word

There are so many things I have forgot,
That once were much to me, or that were not,
All lost, as is a childless woman's child
And its child's children, in the undefiled
Abyss of what will never be again.   5
I have forgot, too, names of the mighty men
That fought and lost or won in the old wars,
Of kings and fiends and gods, and most of the stars.
Some things I have forgot that I forget.
But lesser things there are, remembered yet,   10
Than all the others. One name that I have not –
Though 'tis an empty thingless name – forgot
Never can die because Spring after Spring
Some thrushes learn to say it as they sing.
There is always one at midday saying it clear   15
And tart – the name, only the name I hear.
While perhaps I am thinking of the elder scent
That is like food; or while I am content
With the wild rose scent that is like memory,
This name suddenly is cried out to me   20
From somewhere in the bushes by a bird
Over and over again, a pure thrush word.

Haymaking

After night's thunder far away had rolled
The fiery day had a kernel sweet of cold,
And in the perfect blue the clouds uncurled,
Like the first gods before they made the world
And misery, swimming the stormless sea   5
In beauty and in divine gaiety.
The smooth white empty road was lightly strewn
With leaves – the holly's Autumn falls in June –

And fir cones standing up stiff in the heat.
The mill-foot water tumbled white and lit   10
With tossing crystals, happier than any crowd
Of children pouring out of school aloud.
And in the little thickets where a sleeper
For ever might lie lost, the nettle creeper
And garden-warbler sang unceasingly;   15
While over them shrill shrieked in his fierce glee
The swift with wings and tail as sharp and narrow
As if the bow had flown off with the arrow.
Only the scent of woodbine and hay new mown
Travelled the road. In the field sloping down,   20
Park-like, to where its willows showed the brook,
Haymakers rested. The tosser lay forsook
Out in the sun; and the long waggon stood
Without its team: it seemed it never would
Move from the shadow of that single yew.   25
The team, as still, until their task was due,
Beside the labourers enjoyed the shade
That three squat oaks mid-field together made
Upon a circle of grass and weed uncut,
And on the hollow, once a chalk-pit, but   30
Now brimmed with nut and elder-flower so clean.
The men leaned on their rakes, about to begin,
But still. And all were silent. All was old,
This morning time, with a great age untold,
Older than Clare and Cobbett, Morland and Crome,   35
Than, at the field's far edge, the farmer's home,
A white house crouched at the foot of a great tree.
Under the heavens that know not what years be
The men, the beasts, the trees, the implements
Uttered even what they will in times far hence –   40
All of us gone out of the reach of change –
Immortal in a picture of an old grange.

A Dream

Over known fields with an old friend in dream
I walked, but came sudden to a strange stream.
Its dark waters were bursting out most bright
From a great mountain's heart into the light.
They ran a short course under the sun, then back   5
Into a pit they plunged, once more as black
As at their birth; and I stood thinking there
How white, had the day shone on them, they were,
Heaving and coiling. So by the roar and hiss
And by the mighty motion of the abyss   10
I was bemused, that I forgot my friend
And neither saw nor sought him till the end,
When I awoke from waters unto men
Saying: 'I shall be here some day again.'

The Brook

Seated once by a brook, watching a child
Chiefly that paddled, I was thus beguiled.
Mellow the blackbird sang and sharp the thrush
Not far off in the oak and hazel brush,
Unseen. There was a scent like honeycomb   5
From mugwort dull. And down upon the dome
Of the stone the cart-horse kicks against so oft
A butterfly alighted. From aloft
He took the heat of the sun, and from below.
On the hot stone he perched contented so,   10
As if never a cart would pass again
That way; as if I were the last of men
And he the first of insects to have earth
And sun together and to know their worth.
I was divided between him and the gleam,   15
The motion, and the voices, of the stream,
The waters running frizzled over gravel,

That never vanish and for ever travel.
A grey flycatcher silent on a fence
And I sat as if we had been there since   20
The horseman and the horse lying beneath
The fir-tree-covered barrow on the heath,
The horseman and the horse with silver shoes,
Galloped the downs last. All that I could lose
I lost. And then the child's voice raised the dead.   25
'No one's been here before' was what she said
And what I felt, yet never should have found
A word for, while I gathered sight and sound.

Aspens

All day and night, save winter, every weather,
Above the inn, the smithy, and the shop,
The aspens at the cross-roads talk together
Of rain, until their last leaves fall from the top.

Out of the blacksmith's cavern comes the ringing   5
Of hammer, shoe, and anvil; out of the inn
The clink, the hum, the roar, the random singing –
The sounds that for these fifty years have been.

The whisper of the aspens is not drowned,
And over lightless pane and footless road,   10
Empty as sky, with every other sound
Not ceasing, calls their ghosts from their abode,

A silent smithy, a silent inn, nor fails
In the bare moonlight or the thick-furred gloom,
In tempest or the night of nightingales,   15
To turn the cross-roads to a ghostly room.

And it would be the same were no house near.
Over all sorts of weather, men, and times,

Aspens must shake their leaves and men may hear
But need not listen, more than to my rhymes.   20

Whatever wind blows, while they and I have leaves
We cannot other than an aspen be
That ceaselessly, unreasonably grieves,
Or so men think who like a different tree.

The Mill-Water

Only the sound remains
Of the old mill;
Gone is the wheel;
On the prone roof and walls the nettle reigns.

Water that toils no more   5
Dangles white locks
And, falling, mocks
The music of the mill-wheel's busy roar.

Pretty to see, by day
Its sound is naught   10
Compared with thought
And talk and noise of labour and of play.

Night makes the difference.
In calm moonlight,
Gloom infinite,   15
The sound comes surging in upon the sense:

Solitude, company, –
When it is night, –
Grief or delight
By it must haunted or concluded be.   20

Often the silentness
Has but this one
Companion;
Wherever one creeps in the other is:

Sometimes a thought is drowned   25
By it, sometimes
Out of it climbs;
All thoughts begin or end upon this sound,

Only the idle foam
Of water falling   30
Changelessly calling,
Where once men had a work-place and a home.

For These

An acre of land between the shore and the hills,
Upon a ledge that shows my kingdoms three,
The lovely visible earth and sky and sea
Where what the curlew needs not, the farmer tills:

A house that shall love me as I love it,   5
Well-hedged, and honoured by a few ash trees
That linnets, greenfinches, and goldfinches
Shall often visit and make love in and flit:

A garden I need never go beyond,
Broken but neat, whose sunflowers every one   10
Are fit to be the sign of the Rising Sun:
A spring, a brook's bend, or at least a pond:

For these I ask not, but, neither too late
Nor yet too early, for what men call content,

And also that something may be sent   15
To be contented with, I ask of Fate.

Digging [2]

What matter makes my spade for tears or mirth,
Letting down two clay pipes into the earth?
The one I smoked, the other a soldier
Of Blenheim, Ramillies, and Malplaquet
Perhaps. The dead man's immortality   5
Lies represented lightly with my own,
A yard or two nearer the living air
Than bones of ancients who, amazed to see
Almighty God erect the mastodon,
Once laughed, or wept, in this same light of day.   10

Two Houses

Between a sunny bank and the sun
The farmhouse smiles
On the riverside plat:
No other one
So pleasant to look at   5
And remember, for many miles,
So velvet hushed and cool under the warm tiles.

Not far from the road it lies, yet caught
Far out of reach
Of the road's dust   10
And the dusty thought
Of passers-by, though each
Stops, and turns, and must
Look down at it like a wasp at the muslined peach.

But another house stood there long before: 15
And as if above graves
Still the turf heaves
Above its stones:
Dark hangs the sycamore,
Shadowing kennel and bones   20
And the black dog that shakes his chain and moans.

And when he barks, over the river
Flashing fast,
Dark echoes reply,
And the hollow past   25
Half yields the dead that never
More than half hidden lie:
And out they creep and back again for ever.

Cock-Crow

Out of the wood of thoughts that grows by night
To be cut down by the sharp axe of light, –
Out of the night, two cocks together crow,
Cleaving the darkness with a silver blow:
And bright before my eyes twin trumpeters stand,   5
Heralds of splendour, one at either hand,
Each facing each as in a coat of arms:
The milkers lace their boots up at the farms.

October

The green elm with the one great bough of gold
Lets leaves into the grass slip, one by one, –
The short hill grass, the mushrooms small, milk-white,
Harebell and scabious and tormentil,

That blackberry and gorse, in dew and sun,   5
Bow down to; and the wind travels too light
To shake the fallen birch leaves from the fern;
The gossamers wander at their own will.
At heavier steps than birds' the squirrels scold.
The rich scene has grown fresh again and new   10
As Spring and to the touch is not more cool
Than it is warm to the gaze; and now I might
As happy be as earth is beautiful,
Were I some other or with earth could turn
In alternation of violet and rose,   15
Harebell and snowdrop, at their season due,
And gorse that has no time not to be gay.
But if this be not happiness, – who knows?
Some day I shall think this a happy day,
And this mood by the name of melancholy   20
Shall no more blackened and obscurèd be.

There's Nothing Like the Sun

There's nothing like the sun as the year dies,
Kind as it can be, this world being made so,
To stones and men and beasts and birds and flies,
To all things that it touches except snow,
Whether on mountain side or street of town.   5
The south wall warms me: November has begun,
Yet never shone the sun as fair as now
While the sweet last-left damsons from the bough
With spangles of the morning's storm drop down
Because the starling shakes it, whistling what   10
Once swallows sang. But I have not forgot
That there is nothing, too, like March's sun,
Like April's, or July's, or June's, or May's,
Or January's, or February's, great days:
August, September, October, and December   15
Have equal days, all different from November.

No day of any month but I have said –
Or, if I could live long enough, should say –
'There's nothing like the sun that shines today.'
There's nothing like the sun till we are dead.   20

The Thrush

When Winter's ahead,
What can you read in November
That you read in April
When Winter's dead?

I hear the thrush, and I see   5
Him alone at the end of the lane
Near the bare poplar's tip,
Singing continuously.

Is it more that you know
Than that, even as in April,   10
So in November,
Winter is gone that must go?

Or is all your lore
Not to call November November,
And April April,   15
And Winter Winter – no more?

But I know the months all,
And their sweet names, April,
May and June and October,
As you call and call   20

I must remember
What died in April
And consider what will be born
Of a fair November;

And April I love for what   25
It was born of, and November
For what it will die in,
What they are and what they are not,

While you love what is kind,
What you can sing in   30
And love and forget in
All that's ahead and behind.

Liberty

The last light has gone out of the world, except
This moonlight lying on the grass like frost
Beyond the brink of the tall elm's shadow.
It is as if everything else had slept
Many an age, unforgotten and lost –   5
The men that were, the things done, long ago,
All I have thought; and but the moon and I
Live yet and here stand idle over a grave
Where all is buried. Both have liberty
To dream what we could do if we were free   10
To do some thing we had desired long,
The moon and I. There's none less free than who
Does nothing and has nothing else to do,
Being free only for what is not to his mind,
And nothing is to his mind. If every hour   15
Like this one passing that I have spent among
The wiser others when I have forgot
To wonder whether I was free or not,
Were piled before me, and not lost behind,
And I could take and carry them away   20
I should be rich; or if I had the power
To wipe out every one and not again
Regret, I should be rich to be so poor.
And yet I still am half in love with pain,

With what is imperfect, with both tears and mirth,   25
With things that have an end, with life and earth,
And this moon that leaves me dark within the door.

This is No Case of
Petty Right or Wrong

This is no case of petty right or wrong
That politicians or philosophers
Can judge. I hate not Germans, nor grow hot
With love of Englishmen, to please newspapers.
Beside my hate for one fat patriot   5
My hatred of the Kaiser is love true: –
A kind of god he is, banging a gong.
But I have not to choose between the two,
Or between justice and injustice. Dinned
With war and argument I read no more   10
Than in the storm smoking along the wind
Athwart the wood. Two witches' cauldrons roar.
From one the weather shall rise clear and gay;
Out of the other an England beautiful
And like her mother that died yesterday.   15
Little I know or care if, being dull,
I shall miss something that historians
Can rake out of the ashes when perchance
The phœnix broods serene above their ken.
But with the best and meanest Englishmen   20
I am one in crying, God save England, lest
We lose what never slaves and cattle blessed.
The ages made her that made us from dust:
She is all we know and live by, and we trust
She is good and must endure, loving her so: 25
And as we love ourselves we hate her foe.

1916

Rain

Rain, midnight rain, nothing but the wild rain
On this bleak hut, and solitude, and me
Remembering again that I shall die
And neither hear the rain nor give it thanks
For washing me cleaner than I have been   5
Since I was born into this solitude.
Blessed are the dead that the rain rains upon:
But here I pray that none whom once I loved
Is dying tonight or lying still awake
Solitary, listening to the rain,   10
Either in pain or thus in sympathy
Helpless among the living and the dead,
Like a cold water among broken reeds,
Myriads of broken reeds all still and stiff,
Like me who have no love which this wild rain 15
Has not dissolved except the love of death,
If love it be for what is perfect and
Cannot, the tempest tells me, disappoint.

Roads

I love roads:
The goddesses that dwell
Far along invisible
Are my favourite gods.

Roads go on   5
While we forget, and are

Forgotten like a star
That shoots and is gone.

On this earth 'tis sure
We men have not made   10
Anything that doth fade
So soon, so long endure:

The hill road wet with rain
In the sun would not gleam
Like a winding stream   15
If we trod it not again.

They are lonely
While we sleep, lonelier
For lack of the traveller
Who is now a dream only.   20

From dawn's twilight
And all the clouds like sheep
On the mountains of sleep
They wind into the night.

The next turn may reveal   25
Heaven: upon the crest
The close pine clump, at rest
And black, may Hell conceal.

Often footsore, never
Yet of the road I weary,   30
Though long and steep and dreary,
As it winds on for ever.

Helen of the roads,
The mountain ways of Wales
And the Mabinogion tales   35
Is one of the true gods,

Abiding in the trees,
The threes and fours so wise,

The larger companies,
That by the roadside be,   40

And beneath the rafter
Else uninhabited
Excepting by the dead;
And it is her laughter

At morn and night I hear   45
When the thrush cock sings
Bright irrelevant things,
And when the chanticleer

Calls back to their own night
Troops that make loneliness   50
With their light footsteps' press,
As Helen's own are light.

Now all roads lead to France
And heavy is the tread
Of the living; but the dead   55
Returning lightly dance:

Whatever the road bring
To me or take from me,
They keep me company
With their pattering,   60

Crowding the solitude
Of the loops over the downs,
Hushing the roar of towns
And their brief multitude.

February Afternoon

Men heard this roar of parleying starlings, saw,
  A thousand years ago even as now,
  Black rooks with white gulls following the plough
So that the first are last until a caw
Commands that last are first again, – a law   5
  Which was of old when one, like me, dreamed how
  A thousand years might dust lie on his brow
Yet thus would birds do between hedge and shaw.

Time swims before me, making as a day
  A thousand years, while the broad ploughland oak   10
  Roars mill-like and men strike and bear the stroke
  Of war as ever, audacious or resigned,
And God still sits aloft in the array
  That we have wrought him, stone-deaf and stone-blind.

P. H. T.

I may come near loving you
When you are dead
And there is nothing to do
And much to be said.

To repent that day will be   5
Impossible
For you and vain for me
The truth to tell.

I shall be sorry for
Your impotence: 10

You can do and undo no more
When you go hence,

Cannot even forgive
The funeral.
But not so long as you live   15
Can I love you at all.

These Things that Poets Said

These things that poets said
Of love seemed true to me
When I loved and I fed
On love and poetry equally.

But now I wish I knew   5
If theirs were love indeed,
Or if mine were the true
And theirs some other lovely weed:

For certainly not thus,
Then or thereafter, I   10
Loved ever. Between us
Decide, good Love, before I die.

Only, that once I loved
By this one argument
Is very plainly proved: 15
I, loving not, am different.

No One So Much As You

No one so much as you
Loves this my clay,
Or would lament as you
Its dying day.

You know me through and through   5
Though I have not told,
And though with what you know
You are not bold.

None ever was so fair
As I thought you: 10
Not a word can I bear
Spoken against you.

All that I ever did
For you seemed coarse
Compared with what I hid   15
Nor put in force.

My eyes scarce dare meet you
Lest they should prove
I but respond to you
And do not love.   20

We look and understand,
We cannot speak
Except in trifles and
Words the most weak.

For I at most accept   25
Your love, regretting
That is all: I have kept
Only a fretting

That I could not return
All that you gave   30

And could not ever burn
With the love you have,

Till sometimes it did seem
Better it were
Never to see you more   35
Than linger here

With only gratitude
Instead of love –
A pine in solitude
Cradling a dove.   40

Celandine

Thinking of her had saddened me at first,
Until I saw the sun on the celandines lie
Redoubled, and she stood up like a flame,
A living thing, not what before I nursed,
The shadow I was growing to love almost,   5
The phantom, not the creature with bright eye
That I had thought never to see, once lost.

She found the celandines of February
Always before us all. Her nature and name
Were like those flowers, and now immediately   10
For a short swift eternity back she came,
Beautiful, happy, simply as when she wore
Her brightest bloom among the winter hues
Of all the world; and I was happy too,
Seeing the blossoms and the maiden who   15
Had seen them with me Februarys before,
Bending to them as in and out she trod
And laughed, with locks sweeping the mossy sod.

But this was a dream: the flowers were not true,
Until I stooped to pluck from the grass there   20

One of five petals and I smelt the juice
Which made me sigh, remembering she was no more,
Gone like a never perfectly recalled air.

'Home' [3]

Fair was the morning, fair our tempers, and
We had seen nothing fairer than that land,
Though strange, and the untrodden snow that made
Wild of the tame, casting out all that was
Not wild and rustic and old; and we were glad.   5

Fair too was afternoon, and first to pass
Were we that league of snow, next the north wind.

There was nothing to return for, except need,
And yet we sang nor ever stopped for speed,
As we did often with the start behind.   10
Faster still strode we when we came in sight
Of the cold roofs where we must spend the night.
Happy we had not been there, nor could be,
Though we had tasted sleep and food and fellowship
Together long.

             'How quick', to someone's lip   15
The words came, 'will the beaten horse run home!'

The word 'home' raised a smile in us all three,
And one repeated it, smiling just so
That all knew what he meant and none would say.
Between three counties far apart that lay   20
We were divided and looked strangely each
At the other, and we knew we were not friends
But fellows in a union that ends
With the necessity for it, as it ought.

Never a word was spoken, not a thought   25
Was thought, of what the look meant with the word
'Home' as we walked and watched the sunset blurred.
And then to me the word, only the word,
'Homesick', as it were playfully occurred:
No more.

        If I should ever more admit   30
Than the mere word I could not endure it
For a day longer: this captivity
Must somehow come to an end, else I should be
Another man, as often now I seem,
Or this life be only an evil dream.   35

Thaw

Over the land freckled with snow half-thawed
The speculating rooks at their nests cawed
And saw from elm-tops, delicate as flower of grass,
What we below could not see, Winter pass.

If I Should Ever by Chance

If I should ever by chance grow rich
I'll buy Codham, Cockridden, and Childerditch,
Roses, Pyrgo, and Lapwater,
And let them all to my elder daughter.
The rent I shall ask of her will be only   5
Each year's first violets, white and lonely,
The first primroses and orchises –

She must find them before I do, that is.
But if she finds a blossom on furze
Without rent they shall all for ever be hers,   10
Whenever I am sufficiently rich:
Codham, Cockridden, and Childerditch,
Roses, Pyrgo and Lapwater, –
I shall give them all to my elder daughter.

If I were to Own

If I were to own this countryside
As far as a man in a day could ride,
And the Tyes were mine for giving or letting, –
Wingle Tye and Margaretting
Tye, – and Skreens, Gooshays, and Cockerells,   5
Shellow, Rochetts, Bandish, and Pickerells,
Martins, Lambkins, and Lillyputs,
Their copses, ponds, roads, and ruts,
Fields where plough-horses steam and plovers
Fling and whimper, hedges that lovers   10
Love, and orchards, shrubberies, walls
Where the sun untroubled by north wind falls,
And single trees where the thrush sings well
His proverbs untranslatable,
I would give them all to my son   15
If he would let me any one
For a song, a blackbird's song, at dawn.
He should have no more, till on my lawn
Never a one was left, because I
Had shot them to put them into a pie, –   20
His Essex blackbirds, every one,
And I was left old and alone.

Then unless I could pay, for rent, a song
As sweet as a blackbird's, and as long –
No more – he should have the house, not I   25

Margaretting or Wingle Tye,
Or it might be Skreens, Gooshays, or Cockerells,
Shellow, Rochetts, Bandish, or Pickerells,
Martins, Lambkins, or Lillyputs,
Should be his till the cart tracks had no ruts.   30

What Shall I Give?

What shall I give my daughter the younger
More than will keep her from cold and hunger?
I shall not give her anything.
If she shared South Weald and Havering,
Their acres, the two brooks running between,   5
Paine's Brook and Weald Brook,
With pewit, woodpecker, swan, and rook,
She would be no richer than the queen
Who once on a time sat in Havering Bower
Alone, with the shadows, pleasure and power.   10
She could do no more with Samarcand,
Or the mountains of a mountain land
And its far white house above cottages
Like Venus above the Pleiades.
Her small hands I would not cumber   15
With so many acres and their lumber,
But leave her Steep and her own world
And her spectacled self with hair uncurled,
Wanting a thousand little things
That time without contentment brings.   20

And You, Helen

And you, Helen, what should I give you?
So many things I would give you
Had I an infinite great store
Offered me and I stood before
To choose. I would give you youth,   5
All kinds of loveliness and truth,
A clear eye as good as mine,
Lands, waters, flowers, wine,
As many children as your heart
Might wish for, a far better art   10
Than mine can be, all you have lost
Upon the travelling waters tossed,
Or given to me. If I could choose
Freely in that great treasure-house
Anything from any shelf,   15
I would give you back yourself,
And power to discriminate
What you want and want it not too late,
Many fair days free from care
And heart to enjoy both foul and fair,   20
And myself, too, if I could find
Where it lay hidden and it proved kind.

Like the Touch of Rain

Like the touch of rain she was
On a man's flesh and hair and eyes
When the joy of walking thus
Has taken him by surprise:

With the love of the storm he burns,   5
He sings, he laughs, well I know how,

But forgets when he returns
As I shall not forget her 'Go now'.

Those two words shut a door
Between me and the blessed rain   10
That was never shut before
And will not open again.

When We Two Walked

When we two walked in Lent
We imagined that happiness
Was something different
And this was something less.

But happy were we to hide   5
Our happiness, not as they were
Who acted in their pride
Juno and Jupiter:

For the Gods in their jealousy
Murdered that wife and man,   10
And we that were wise live free
To recall our happiness then.

Tall Nettles

Tall nettles cover up, as they have done
These many springs, the rusty harrow, the plough
Long worn out, and the roller made of stone:
Only the elm butt tops the nettles now.

This corner of the farmyard I like most: 5
As well as any bloom upon a flower
I like the dust on the nettles, never lost
Except to prove the sweetness of a shower.

The Watchers

By the ford at the town's edge
Horse and carter rest:
The carter smokes on the bridge
Watching the water press in swathes about his horse's chest.

From the inn one watches, too,   5
In the room for visitors
That has no fire, but a view
And many cases of stuffed fish, vermin, and kingfishers.

I Never Saw that Land Before

I never saw that land before,
And now can never see it again;
Yet, as if by acquaintance hoar
Endeared, by gladness and by pain,
Great was the affection that I bore   5

To the valley and the river small,
The cattle, the grass, the bare ash trees,
The chickens from the farmsteads, all
Elm-hidden, and the tributaries
Descending at equal interval;   10

The blackthorns down along the brook
With wounds yellow as crocuses

Where yesterday the labourer's hook
Had sliced them cleanly; and the breeze
That hinted all and nothing spoke.   15

I neither expected anything
Nor yet remembered: but some goal
I touched then; and if I could sing
What would not even whisper my soul
As I went on my journeying,   20

I should use, as the trees and birds did,
A language not to be betrayed;
And what was hid should still be hid
Excepting from those like me made
Who answer when such whispers bid.   25

The Cherry Trees

The cherry trees bend over and are shedding,
On the old road where all that passed are dead,
Their petals, strewing the grass as for a wedding
This early May morn when there is none to wed.

It Rains

It rains, and nothing stirs within the fence
Anywhere through the orchard's untrodden, dense
Forest of parsley. The great diamonds
Of rain on the grassblades there is none to break,
Or the fallen petals further down to shake.   5

And I am nearly as happy as possible
To search the wilderness in vain though well,

To think of two walking, kissing there,
Drenched, yet forgetting the kisses of the rain:
Sad, too, to think that never, never again,   10

Unless alone, so happy shall I walk
In the rain. When I turn away, on its fine stalk
Twilight has fined to naught, the parsley flower
Figures, suspended still and ghostly white,
The past hovering as it revisits the light.   15

The Sun Used to Shine

The sun used to shine while we two walked
Slowly together, paused and started
Again, and sometimes mused, sometimes talked
As either pleased, and cheerfully parted

Each night. We never disagreed   5
Which gate to rest on. The to be
And the late past we gave small heed.
We turned from men or poetry

To rumours of the war remote
Only till both stood disinclined   10
For aught but the yellow flavorous coat
Of an apple wasps had undermined;

Or a sentry of dark betonies,
The stateliest of small flowers on earth,
At the forest verge; or crocuses   15
Pale purple as if they had their birth

In sunless Hades fields. The war
Came back to mind with the moonrise
Which soldiers in the east afar
Beheld then. Nevertheless, our eyes   20

Could as well imagine the Crusades
Or Cæsar's battles. Everything
To faintness like those rumours fades –
Like the brook's water glittering

Under the moonlight – like those walks   25
Now – like us two that took them, and
The fallen apples, all the talks
And silences – like memory's sand

When the tide covers it late or soon,
And other men through other flowers   30
In those fields under the same moon
Go talking and have easy hours.

No One Cares Less than I

'No one cares less than I,
Nobody knows but God,
Whether I am destined to lie
Under a foreign clod,'
Were the words I made to the bugle call in the morning.   5

But laughing, storming, scorning,
Only the bugles know
What the bugles say in the morning,
And they do not care, when they blow
The call that I heard and made words to early this morning.   10

As the Team's Head-Brass

As the team's head-brass flashed out on the turn
The lovers disappeared into the wood.
I sat among the boughs of the fallen elm
That strewed the angle of the fallow, and
Watched the plough narrowing a yellow square   5
Of charlock. Every time the horses turned
Instead of treading me down, the ploughman leaned
Upon the handles to say or ask a word,
About the weather, next about the war.
Scraping the share he faced towards the wood,   10
And screwed along the furrow till the brass flashed
Once more.
        The blizzard felled the elm whose crest
I sat in, by a woodpecker's round hole,
The ploughman said. 'When will they take it away?'
'When the war's over.' So the talk began –   15
One minute and an interval of ten,
A minute more and the same interval.
'Have you been out?' 'No.' 'And don't want to, perhaps?'
'If I could only come back again, I should.
I could spare an arm. I shouldn't want to lose   20
A leg. If I should lose my head, why, so,
I should want nothing more. . . . Have many gone
From here?' 'Yes.' 'Many lost?' 'Yes, a good few.
Only two teams work on the farm this year.
One of my mates is dead. The second day   25
In France they killed him. It was back in March,
The very night of the blizzard, too. Now if
He had stayed here we should have moved the tree.'
'And I should not have sat here. Everything
Would have been different. For it would have been   30
Another world.' 'Ay, and a better, though
If we could see all all might seem good.' Then
The lovers came out of the wood again:
The horses started and for the last time
I watched the clods crumble and topple over   35
After the ploughshare and the stumbling team.

Bright Clouds

Bright clouds of may
Shade half the pond.
Beyond,
All but one bay
Of emerald   5
Tall reeds
Like criss-cross bayonets
Where a bird once called,
Lies bright as the sun.
No one heeds.   10
The light wind frets
And drifts the scum
Of may-blossom.
Till the moorhen calls
Again   15
Naught's to be done
By birds or men.
Still the may falls.

It Was Upon

It was upon a July evening.
At a stile I stood, looking along a path
Over the country by a second Spring
Drenched perfect green again. 'The lattermath
Will be a fine one.' So the stranger said,   5
A wandering man. Albeit I stood at rest,
Flushed with desire I was. The earth outspread,
Like meadows of the future, I possessed.

And as an unaccomplished prophecy
The stranger's words, after the interval   10
Of a score years, when those fields are by me

Never to be recrossed, now I recall,
This July eve, and question, wondering,
What of the lattermath to this hoar Spring?

There Was a Time

There was a time when this poor frame was whole
And I had youth and never another care,
Or none that should have troubled a strong soul.
Yet, except sometimes in a frosty air
When my heels hammered out a melody   5
From pavements of a city left behind,
I never would acknowledge my own glee
Because it was less mighty than my mind
Had dreamed of. Since I could not boast of strength
Great as I wished, weakness was all my boast.   10
I sought yet hated pity till at length
I earned it. Oh, too heavy was the cost!
But now that there is something I could use
My youth and strength for, I deny the age,
The care and weakness that I know – refuse   15
To admit I am unworthy of the wage
Paid to a man who gives up eyes and breath
For what would neither ask nor heed his death.

The Green Roads

The green roads that end in the forest
Are strewn with white goose feathers this June,

Like marks left behind by someone gone to the forest
To show his track. But he has never come back.

Down each green road a cottage looks at the forest.   5
Round one the nettle towers; two are bathed in flowers.

An old man along the green road to the forest
Strays from one, from another a child alone.

In the thicket bordering the forest,
All day long a thrush twiddles his song.   10

It is old, but the trees are young in the forest,
All but one like a castle keep, in the middle deep.

That oak saw the ages pass in the forest:
They were a host, but their memories are lost,

For the tree is dead: all things forget the forest   15
Excepting perhaps me, when now I see

The old man, the child, the goose feathers at the edge of the
    forest,
And hear all day long the thrush repeat his song.

When First

When first I came here I had hope,
Hope for I knew not what. Fast beat
My heart at sight of the tall slope
Of grass and yews, as if my feet

Only by scaling its steps of chalk   5
Would see something no other hill
Ever disclosed. And now I walk
Down it the last time. Never will

My heart beat so again at sight
Of any hill although as fair   10

And loftier. For infinite
The change, late unperceived, this year,

The twelfth, suddenly, shows me plain.
Hope now, – not health, nor cheerfulness,
Since they can come and go again,   15
As often one brief hour witnesses, –

Just hope has gone for ever. Perhaps
I may love other hills yet more
Than this: the future and the maps
Hide something I was waiting for.   20

One thing I know, that love with chance
And use and time and necessity
Will grow, and louder the heart's dance
At parting than at meeting be.

The Gallows

There was a weasel lived in the sun
With all his family,
Till a keeper shot him with his gun
And hung him up on a tree,
Where he swings in the wind and rain,   5
In the sun and in the snow,
Without pleasure, without pain,
On the dead oak tree bough.

There was a crow who was no sleeper,
But a thief and a murderer   10
Till a very late hour; and this keeper
Made him one of the things that were,
To hang and flap in rain and wind,
In the sun and in the snow.

There are no more sins to be sinned   15
On the dead oak tree bough.

There was a magpie, too,
Had a long tongue and a long tail;
He could both talk and do –
But what did that avail?   20
He, too, flaps in the wind and rain
Alongside weasel and crow,
Without pleasure, without pain,
On the dead oak tree bough.

And many other beasts   25
And birds, skin, bone, and feather,
Have been taken from their feasts
And hung up there together,
To swing and have endless leisure
In the sun and in the snow,   30
Without pain, without pleasure,
On the dead oak tree bough.

The Dark Forest

Dark is the forest and deep, and overhead
Hang stars like seeds of light
In vain, though not since they were sown was bred
Anything more bright.

And evermore mighty multitudes ride   5
About, nor enter in;
Of the other multitudes that dwell inside
Never yet was one seen.

The forest foxglove is purple, the marguerite
Outside is gold and white,   10
Nor can those that pluck either blossom greet
The others, day or night.

How at Once

How at once should I know,
When stretched in the harvest blue
I saw the swift's black bow,
That I would not have that view
Another day   5
Until next May
Again it is due?

The same year after year –
But with the swift alone.
With other things I but fear   10
That they will be over and done
Suddenly
And I only see
Them to know them gone.

Gone, Gone Again

Gone, gone again,
May, June, July,
And August gone,
Again gone by,

Not memorable   5
Save that I saw them go,
As past the empty quays
The rivers flow.

And now again,
In the harvest rain,   10
The Blenheim oranges
Fall grubby from the trees

As when I was young –
And when the lost one was here –
And when the war began   15
To turn young men to dung.

Look at the old house,
Outmoded, dignified,
Dark and untenanted,
With grass growing instead   20

Of the footsteps of life,
The friendliness, the strife;
In its beds have lain
Youth, love, age, and pain:

I am something like that;   25
Only I am not dead,
Still breathing and interested
In the house that is not dark: –

I am something like that:
Not one pane to reflect the sun,   30
For the schoolboys to throw at –
They have broken every one.

What Will They Do?

What will they do when I am gone? It is plain
That they will do without me as the rain
Can do without the flowers and the grass
That profit by it and must perish without.
I have but seen them in the loud street pass;   5
And I was naught to them. I turned about
To see them disappearing carelessly.
But what if I in them as they in me
Nourished what has great value and no price?

Almost I thought that rain thirsts for a draught   10
Which only in the blossom's chalice lies,
Until that one turned back and lightly laughed.

The Trumpet

Rise up, rise up,
And, as the trumpet blowing
Chases the dreams of men,
As the dawn glowing
The stars that left unlit   5
The land and water,
Rise up and scatter
The dew that covers
The print of last night's lovers –
Scatter it, scatter it!   10

While you are listening
To the clear horn,
Forget, men, everything
On this earth new-born,
Except that it is lovelier   15
Than any mysteries.
Open your eyes to the air
That has washed the eyes of the stars
Through all the dewy night:
Up with the light,   20
To the old wars;
Arise, arise!

Lights Out

I have come to the borders of sleep,
The unfathomable deep
Forest where all must lose
Their way, however straight,
Or winding, soon or late;   5
They cannot choose.

Many a road and track
That, since the dawn's first crack,
Up to the forest brink,
Deceived the travellers,   10
Suddenly now blurs,
And in they sink.

Here love ends,
Despair, ambition ends;
All pleasure and all trouble,   15
Although most sweet or bitter,
Here ends in sleep that is sweeter
Than tasks most noble.

There is not any book
Or face of dearest look   20
That I would not turn from now
To go into the unknown
I must enter, and leave, alone,
I know not how.

The tall forest towers;   25
Its cloudy foliage lowers
Ahead, shelf above shelf;
Its silence I hear and obey
That I may lose my way
And myself.   30

Out in the Dark

Out in the dark over the snow
The fallow fawns invisible go
With the fallow doe;
And the winds blow
Fast as the stars are slow.   5

Stealthily the dark haunts round
And, when the lamp goes, without sound
At a swifter bound
Than the swiftest hound,
Arrives, and all else is drowned;   10

And star and I and wind and deer,
Are in the dark together, – near,
Yet far, – and fear
Drums on my ear
In that sage company drear.   15

How weak and little is the light,
All the universe of sight,
Love and delight,
Before the might,
If you love it not, of night   20

1917

Last Poem [The sorrow of true love]

The sorrow of true love is a great sorrow
And true love parting blackens a bright morrow:
Yet almost they equal joys, since their despair
Is but hope blinded by its tears, and clear
Above the storm the heavens wait to be seen.　　　5
But greater sorrow from less love has been
That can mistake lack of despair for hope
And knows not tempest and the perfect scope
Of summer, but a frozen drizzle perpetual
Of drops that from remorse and pity fall　　　　10
And cannot ever shine in the sun or thaw,
Removed eternally from the sun's law.

Notes

Text from Edward Thomas's *Collected Poems* is reprinted by permission of Mrs Myfanwy Thomas. (For the bibliography of *Collected Poems*, see p. xxi.) The date of each poem's composition is given in brackets after the title, although the dating of the five poems marked * is approximate.

Abbreviations: ET: Edward Thomas; HT: Helen Thomas; RF: Robert Frost

1914

Up in the Wind (3 December) **35 'The 'White Horse':** an inn at Froxfield, near Steep.

November (4 December)

March (5 December)

Old Man (6 December)

The Sign-Post (7 December) Cf. RF's 'The Road Not Taken' in which he obliquely parodied ET's more hesitant outlook.

*The Other** (8–13 December 1914 [?]) ET wrote to a friend in 1911: 'my head . . . is almost always wrong now – a sort of conspiracy going on in it which leaves me only a joint tenancy and a perpetual scare of the other tenant and wonder what he will do.' **67 crocketed:** crockets are architectural ornaments, usually like curled leaves.

*Interval** (mid December 1914 [?])

*Birds' Nests** (mid December 1914 [?])

*The Mountain Chapel** (mid December 1914 [?])

The Manor Farm (24 December) **24 This England:** an echo of John of Gaunt's panegyric (Shakespeare, *Richard II*, II.i.50). It is also the title of both an essay by ET and a patriotic anthology he edited (1915) in which he included this poem and 'Haymaking' under the pseudonym of Edward Eastaway.

The Combe (30 December)

The Hollow Wood (31 December)

1915

The New Year (1 January) **19 may it come fastish, too:** an allusion to the war, which in August 1914 had been hailed as 'over by Christmas'.

The Penny Whistle (5 January)

A Private (6 and 7 January and 1 August)

Snow (7 January)

Adlestrop (8 January) The station (now closed) was half a mile from the village of Adlestrop, which is between Stow-on-the-Wold and Chipping Norton. The station's nameboard hangs in the village bus-shelter as a memorial.

Tears (8 January) **6 Blooming Meadow:** a field at Elses Farm, Kent.

Over the Hills (9 January)

The Lofty Sky (10 January) **34 To where the lilies are:** the lilies represent sky, a place of spiritual regeneration. The impulse behind the poem is akin to that of RF in 'Birches': 'I'd like to get away from earth awhile / And then come back to it and begin over.'

Swedes (15 January) **6 Valley of the Tombs of Kings:** a valley near ancient Thebes in Egypt where pharaohs of the New Kingdom were buried. **11 Amen-hotep:** the name of four pharaohs of the eighteenth dynasty, the fourth being father-in-law to Tutankhamen.

The Unknown Bird (17 January)

Man and Dog (20 January) **7 flag-basket:** a reed basket for tools. **10 'a money-box':** some savings. **12 flint-picking:** stone-clearing so that a field can be cultivated.

Beauty (21 January)

The Gypsy (22 January) In *George Borrow* (1912), ET wrote that Borrow was 'a big truculent outdoor wizard, who comes to our doors with a marvellous company of Gypsies and fellows whose like we shall never see again and could not invent'. **17 Bacchanal:** roistering. **20 cheap-jack:**

a seller of inferior goods. **22 the kneeling ox:** an evocation of the Nativity (cf. Hardy's 'The Oxen').

Parting (11 February) Written on the day ET's son left with the Frosts for America. As with his own father, ET's relations with Merfyn were somewhat strained.

First Known when Lost (11 February)

May the Twenty-third (15 February) **46 Noman:** see 'Lob', line 138.

The Barn (22 February)

Home [1] (23 February) Cf. George Herbert's poem 'Home' (which ET included in his 1908 edition of Herbert's verse). **Verses 3 and 4:** cf. Hamlet's 'To be or not to be' soliloquy (Shakespeare, *Hamlet*, III.i.79–82).

The Owl (24 February) **10 No merry note:** an allusion to the song at the end of Shakespeare's *Love's Labour's Lost*: 'then nightly sings the staring owl: "Tu-who; / Tu-whit, Tu-who" – a merry note'. **13 salted:** '*flavoured* or *spiced*, but at the same time less comfortable connotations are invoked; the harshness of salt, the salt in the wound, the taste of bitterness and of tears' (Vernon Scannell, *Edward Thomas*, *Writers and their Work*, no. 163, pp. 19–20).

The Bridge (12 March)

But These Things Also (18 March)

The New House (19 March) **Title:** the house at Wick Green into which the Thomases moved in 1909 and in which ET suffered a severe breakdown. The house also features in 'Wind and Mist'.

Sowing (23 March)

Two Pewits (24 March)

The Path (26 March)

A Tale (28 March) A revised version (dated 31 March) is also extant.

Wind and Mist (1 April) See note on 'The New House' above.

Lob (3 and 4 April) **Title:** Lob a.k.a. Hob, Robin Goodfellow, Puck (cf. 'thou lob of spirits' in Shakespeare's *A Midsummer Night's Dream*, II.i.16). **10 scaring sparrows:** children were employed to scare birds away from the seed. **14–17 three Manningfords ... Alton Priors:** villages in Wiltshire. **26 shot the weathercock:** a traditionally foolish act. **38 the**

White Horse: a horse on a hillside formed by removing the turf from the underlying chalk. **65 herbal Gerard:** John Gerard (1545–1612) whose *Herball* was published in 1597. **68 Jan Toy:** Lob's sweetheart; **"Pretty dear":** traditional version of the blackbird's song (cf. Hardy's 'The Spring Call'). **74 Mother Dunch's Buttocks:** a local name for Sinodun Hill, Berkshire. **76 Totteridge . . . Juggler's Lane:** places in Hertfordshire and Wiltshire. **96–8 tall Tom . . . by the wall:** another reference to the song at the end of *Love's Labour's Lost*. **99 Herne the Hunter:** a former keeper in Windsor Park said to haunt it still (see Shakespeare, *The Merry Wives of Windsor*, IV.iv.27ff). ET related the story in his *Windsor Castle* (1910). **113–22:** ET included this story, from Charlotte S. Burne's *Shropshire Folk Lore*, in his *This England* anthology. Behind the image of the giant as the archetypal invader may lie the German threat. In his contemporaneous essay 'It's a Long, Long Way', ET reported that country people worried about invasion: 'Napoleon, a hundred years ago, was expected to sail up the Severn and destroy the Forest: now it was feared that the Germans were coming.' **123 Gotham:** a village in Nottingham famed for the stupidity of its inhabitants. **133 Jack Cade:** leader of a popular rising against Henry VI in 1450. **136 Jack-in-the-hedge . . . Robin-run-by-the-wall:** names given to several plants. **137 Robin Hood:** semi-legendary medieval outlaw after whom various plants are named, including **Ragged Robin**. **138 No Man's Land:** originally unowned wasteland; more recently the space between opposing armies. **146 old-man's-beard:** the plant 'traveller's joy'. **149–50 Wiltshireman . . . began:** the 'old man' in line 3 may be based on David Uzzell, a Wiltshire countryman ET had known since boyhood; his successor, the squire's son, may recall the Wiltshireman Richard Jefferies (1848–87), an account of whose life ET published in 1909.

Digging [1] (4 April)

Lovers (5 April)

In Memoriam (Easter, 1915) (6 April)

Head and Bottle (14 April)

Home [2] (17 April)

Health (18 April) **31 Alcibiades:** Athenian general and statesman (*c.* 450–404 BC). **32 Mazeppa:** hetman of the Cossacks in the Russian Ukraine (1644?–1709), known to ET through Byron's poem of this title.

Melancholy (25 April)

The Glory* (6 May 1915 [?])

July (7 May)

The Chalk-Pit (8 May) **35–51 I used to meet a man ... breed:** probably one of the many wry self-portraits scattered in ET's prose and poetry. The girl recalls the young HT. **53–4 I should prefer the truth / Or nothing:** the two voices in the poem may represent two sides of ET, the romantic fantasist (evident in some of his earlier prose books) and the plain speaker who, preferring an unvarnished reality, yet responds to a more genuine and profound mystery. Cf. 'Sedge-Warblers'.

Fifty Faggots (13 May)

Sedge-Warblers (23 May)

I Built Myself a House of Glass (25 May)

Words (26–8 June) **45–6 Whose nightingales / Have no wings:** the musical Welsh people.

The Word (5 July)

Haymaking (6–8 July) **35 Clare ... Crome:** John Clare (1793–1864), poet of rural England; William Cobbett (1763–1835), a prolific writer whose *Rural Rides* ET had edited in 1912; George Morland (1763–1804) and John Crome (1768–1821), painters of rural scenes and landscapes.

A Dream (7, 8 July) **1 old friend:** RF. Three days after the poem's composition ET wrote to tell him of his decision to enlist. **9–10 by the roar ... abyss:** suggestions of war and death.

The Brook (10 July)

Aspens (11 July)

The Mill-Water (12 July)

For These (13–14 July) Completed on the day ET was passed medically fit for enlistment.

Digging [2] (21 July) The first poem after ET had enlisted. **4 Blenheim ... :** ET had recently completed his last commissioned work, *The Life of the Duke of Marlborough* (1915). Blenheim (1704), Ramillies (1706) and Malplaquet (1709) were three of Marlborough's victories. **5–10 The dead man's immortality ... light of day:** 'His "digging" or imaginative archaeology uncovers the common humanity, and inhumanity, that links the ages . . . "Almighty God" is semi-ironic; "the mastodon", an image at once awe-inspiring and brutal, suggests the scale and oppression of war.' (Edna Longley, *Poems and Last Poems*, pp.294–5)

Two Houses (22 July)

Cock-Crow (23 July)

October (15–16 October)

There's Nothing Like the Sun (18–19 November)

The Thrush (November)

Liberty (26 November) **24 half in love with pain:** cf. Keats' 'half in love with easeful Death' ('Ode to a Nightingale'). ET's *Keats*, written in 1913, was first published in 1916.

This is No Case of Petty Right or Wrong (26 December)

1916

Rain (7 January)

Roads (22 January) **33–5 Helen . . . tales:** ET provided his own gloss in a letter to Eleanor Farjeon: 'Helen is the lady in the Mabinogion [a collection of medieval Welsh tales], the Welsh lady who married Maxen the Emperor and gave her name to the great old mountain roads – Sarn Helen they are all marked on the maps . . . She is known to mythologists as one of the travelling goddesses of the dusk.' *Edward Thomas, The Last Four Years*, p. 182. That it was also his wife's name was surely no coincidence.

February Afternoon (7 and 8 February) **13–14 And God . . . stone-blind:** A note on the last page of ET's war diary reads: 'I never understood quite what was meant by God.'

P. H. T. (8 February) The initials of ET's father. The poem remained unpublished until 1949.

These Things that Poets Said (9 February)

No One So Much As You (11 February) The poem, addressed to ET's mother, was first published in 1928.

Celandine (4 March) **9–10 name . . . flowers:** 'Helen': 'Celan'dine? The poem may evoke ET's courtship of Helen.

'Home' [3] (7 and 10 March) **12 cold roofs:** the army huts of Hare Hall Camp, near Romford in Essex, where ET was stationed; 'home', applied to them, is in wryly ironic inverted commas.

Thaw (10 March)

If I Should Ever by Chance (29 March – 6 April) **2–3 Codham . . . Lapwater:** the names in this and the next poem are names (of fields, farms, woods, etc.) taken from the country around Hare Hall Camp. **4 elder daughter:** Bronwen (1902–1975).

If I were to Own (1–7 April) **15 my son:** Merfyn (1900–1965).

What Shall I Give? (2–8 April) **1 daughter the younger:** Myfanwy (b. 1910). **8–9 the queen . . . Havering Bower:** Queen Eleanor (widow of Edward I) and Queen Joan (of Henry IV) used the royal residence which was reserved for queens in their widowhood. **11 Samarcand:** usually Samarkand, one of the oldest cities of Asia, a prosperous centre of the silk trade.

And You, Helen (9 April) ET's wife (1877–1967). For her account of their life together, see *As It Was* and *World Without End.*

Like the Touch of Rain (22–30 April)

When We Two Walked (23 April–1 May) **1 we two:** ET and HT. **7–8 Who acted . . . Jupiter:** a reference perhaps to the classical fable of King Ceyx and his Queen Alcyone who aped the king and queen of the gods. Zeus (Jupiter) turned them into birds.

Tall Nettles (24 April–1 May)

The Watchers (24 April–1 May)

I Never Saw that Land Before (5 May)

The Cherry Trees (7–8 May)

It Rains (11–13 May)

The Sun Used to Shine (22 May) **1 we two:** ET and RF. The poem commemorated their 'special relationship' during August 1914 when their two families were close to each other in Ledington. Cf. RF's 'Iris by Night' and 'To ET'. **21–2 Could as well . . . battles:** a suggestion that all wars, whether religious or imperial, are essentially the same. Cf. the 'old wars' ('The Trumpet') and 'February Afternoon'.

No One Cares Less than I (25–6 May)

As the Team's Head-Brass (27 May)

Bright Clouds (4–5 June)

It Was Upon (21 June)

There Was a Time (23 June)

The Green Roads (28 June)

When First (1–2 July) Probably written after ET had had to move his books from his hill-top study down to his cottage in Steep. Soon afterwards the Thomases left Steep. **3 tall slope:** where the ET memorial stone now stands. See Alun Lewis's poem 'To Edward Thomas'.

The Gallows (3–4 July) Written a few days after the start of the Battle of the Somme.

The Dark Forest (1, 5, 10 July)

How at Once (10 August)

Gone, Gone Again (3 September) **11 Blenheim oranges:** golden-coloured apples which ripen late in the season.

What Will They Do? (15 September)

The Trumpet (26–8 [?] September)

Lights Out (November)

Out in the Dark (24 December) Written during Christmas leave at the Thomases' new cottage in Epping Forest.

1917

Last Poem [The sorrow of true love] (13 January) The poem was on the last page of the diary ET kept during his final three months as a soldier. It was first published in 1971.

Everyman's Poetry

Titles available in this series

William Blake
ed. Peter Butter
0 460 87800 X

The Brontës
ed. Pamela Norris
0 460 87864 6

Rupert Brooke & Wilfred Owen
ed. George Walter
0 460 87801 8

Robert Browning
ed. Colin Graham
0 460 87893 X

Robert Burns
ed. Donald Low
0 460 87814 X

Lord Byron
ed. Jane Stabler
0 460 87810 7

Geoffrey Chaucer:
Comic and Bawdy Tales
ed. Malcolm Andrew
0 460 87869 7

John Clare
ed. R. K. R. Thornton
0 460 87823 9

Samuel Taylor Coleridge
ed. John Beer
0 460 87826 3

Emily Dickinson
ed. Helen McNeil
0 460 87895 6

John Donne
ed. D. J. Enright
0 460 87901 4

Four Metaphysical Poets
ed. Douglas Brooks-Davies
0 460 87857 3

Oliver Goldsmith
ed Robert L. Mack
0 460 87827 1

Thomas Gray
ed. Robert L. Mack
0 460 87805 0

Ivor Gurney
ed. George Walter
0 460 87797 6

Heinrich Heine
ed. T. J. Reed & David Cram
0 460 87865 4

George Herbert
ed. D. J. Enright
0 460 87795 X

Robert Herrick
ed. Douglas Brooks-Davies
0 460 87799 2

John Keats
ed. Nicholas Roe
0 460 87808 5

William Shakespeare
ed. Martin Dodsworth
0 460 87815 8

Henry Wadsworth Longfellow
ed. Anthony Thwaite
0 460 87821 2

John Skelton
ed. Greg Walker
0 460 87796 8

Andrew Marvell
ed. Gordon Campbell
0 460 87812 3

R. L. Stevenson
ed. Jenni Calder
0 460 87809 3

John Milton
ed. Gordon Campbell
0 460 87813 1

Algernon Charles Swinburne
ed. Catherine Maxwell
0 460 87871 9

More Poetry Please!
Foreword by P. J. Kavanagh
0 460 87899 9

Alfred, Lord Tennyson
ed. Michael Baron
0 460 87802 6

Edgar Allan Poe
ed. Richard Gray
0 460 87804 2

Dylan Thomas
ed. Walford Davies
0 460 87831 X

Poetry Please!
Foreword by Charles Causley
0 460 87824 7

Edward Thomas
ed. William Cooke
0 460 87877 8

Alexander Pope
ed. Douglas Brooks-Davies
0 460 87798 4

R. S. Thomas
ed. Anthony Thwaite
0 460 87811 5

Alexander Pushkin
ed. A. D. P. Briggs
0 460 87862 X

Walt Whitman
ed. Ellman Crasnow
0 460 87825 5

Lord Rochester
ed. Paddy Lyons
0 460 87819 0

Oscar Wilde
ed. Robert Mighall
0 460 87803 4

Christina Rossetti
ed. Jan Marsh
0 460 87820 4

W. B. Yeats
ed. John Kelly
0 460 87902 2